DATE YOUR WIFE

5-AMBR

DATE YOUR WIFE

THE CRUCIBLE OF RELATIONSHIP

Salvatore V. Ambrosino, M.D.

To order additional copies of this book, contact:
Xlibris Corporation
1-888-7-XLIBRIS
www.Xlibris.com
Orders@Xlibris.com

OTHER WORKS BY

Salvatore V. Ambrosino, M. D.

Twigs for an Eagle's Nest, 1976

The Swelling Tide, 1998

Seams of A Woman's Soul, 1999

To my teachers:
my mother, my wife, my daughters, the women of my practice,
and especially to my grandmother Giuditta Guadagni Di Maio

CONTENTS

5-AMBR

FOREWORD

I n *Date Your Wife: The Crucible of Relationship*, Dr. Salvatore Ambrosino examines the many aspects of marriage and interprets for us the dynamics of how a marriage can become a true union. The couple who is sincerely looking for solutions to forming a true union can find them in the wisdom of Dr. Ambrosino's findings.

There are many things that can go wrong in a relationship. These problems can be resolved if there is true unselfishness one toward the other. This is Love. It is the unselfish giving of one to the other that constitutes true Love. Once focused on the real problems, and the willingness of both partners to give unselfishly of themselves, these problems can be resolved.

The same can be true with same sex unions. While these unions face many of the same problems as heterosexual couples, they face many more problems, i.e. they do not have the same rights nor the legal and medical benefits that are automatically granted to the heterosexual couple. Quite often they do not have the support and understanding that heterosexual couples often have. Despite these social problems, when the love is real and acceptance is there, same sex unions can take place.

Dr. Ambrosino makes it clear that the same sex couple can approach these problems also with the same willingness to give of each other and form and maintain their relationship as a true union.

For a marriage or a life partnership to become a union, unselfish love is the principal catalyst, and the willingness to improve the union is a never ending, but always fulfilling journey.

Dr. Ambrosino's keen insights and perceptive observations are very encouraging, and offer us a truly viable way to keep our unions thriving and vital.

Date Your Wife is the definitive study of the components that transform a relationship into a true union.

Anonymous

FOREWORD

For the divorced person, *Date Your Wife* is a "working through" experience. All the bits and pieces of recalled past attempts for a successful marriage or union are there in bold relief and are to be viewed, reviewed, incorporated, rejected or resolved.

Past feelings and ideas are put in perspective and in the process often help diminish a sense of personal failure. The "mistakes" remain. However, a new sense of appreciation for the struggle to enter the crucible with another develops even as the "should haves/could haves" emerge from the vivid examples and descriptions and highlight what might have been, had good will been present.

The most important and significant focus in this writing is the emphasis on the broad potential present in every relationship to develop into a lasting union. What remains essential is a willingness to sacrifice for love of another. A center to center relatedness is not restricted to husbands and wives only but rather is open to all who in honest spiritual soul-searching reach from within to extend without toward another in loving meaningful connectedness.

Anonymous

FOREWORD

Date Your Wife, Dr. Salvatore Ambrosino's book about striving to create a union of spirit within the context of marriage, is no easy read. This is not a "how-to" or quick fix program so popular in today's culture. He unerringly peels away the fallacious, yet oh so seductive "I deserve to have you make me happy at all costs" approach to marriage that is so prevalent today. This is a book that demands commitment from the reader, along with an acceptance of the personal responsibility that we each must bear in our marriage if it is to grow into something greater than the parts we each bring to it. It requires that the reader be willing to open him or herself up to honest, thoughtful introspection and self-examination if there is to be anything of value gained. What reader does not find him or herself squirming just a little when reading about the caricatured marriages in Chapter 4, "The Paradox of Marriage." Who can honestly deny that some bits and pieces of the portrayal of those couples doesn't hit close to home!

Akin to the Ghost of Christmas Present in Dickens' *A Christmas Carol*, Dr. Ambrosino serves as a spiritual guide who presents an unflinching look at the problems we, as fallible human beings, are faced with in our journey through life and toward love and true communion of spirit. Shining a light on our imperfections, Dr. Ambrosino does not seek to berate or belittle, but rather he seeks to expose our frailties in order that they be understood and in doing so, allowing a foundation of honesty, acceptance, tolerance, patience, and tenderness to take root, so that real intimacy in marriage can flourish.

15

The chapter that deals with dating your wife has perhaps the most easily understood and yet most often ignored piece of practical advice. Dating your spouse seems, at first glance, well, corny. It may be wise to consider that in this country alone we spend countless dollars on picture taking and videos for the express purpose of being able to remember cherished people, events and times in our lives – how can we ever doubt the value of remembrance. The exhortation for couples to actively remember the feeling of when love was new can be a daunting task, when it gets lost so easily and almost silently amid the detritus of everyday living. However, as Dr. Ambrosino points out, this time out, this pause, facilitates conversation and gives us the emotional space necessary to regain our connectedness to our spouse. Its value is inestimable.

In the chapter entitled "The Transformation of Marriage to Union," the reader begins to understand that the crucible of relationship is like the transformation of chrysalis to butterfly, one change engendering another, each new one building upon the last, some too small to even calculate, but without which change cannot occur – there are no short cuts.

On a personal note, I would like to give testimony as to the value of *Date Your Wife* in striving for that transformation of marriage to union and splendor of the Next Day:

Last night I lay in bed on my left side, in my familiar "S" shape. My husband lay behind me, molding himself to me closely, two spoons fitting together – breast to back, pelvis to buttocks, leg to leg, and foot to foot. He draped his arm around me and drew me even closer, squeezing me gently. My silent date – no word was spoken; it was the ultimate intimacy, a wordless hosanna to our love, our union at its simplest yet fullest.

Last night as I lay in bed on my left side, in my familiar "S" shape, the remembrance of my husband's loving touch sustains me still, even these many months after his death.

Loretta Napoli

INTRODUCTION

Decades ago, Chesterton opined that the world would not be lost because of "a lack of wonders" but because of "the loss of a sense of wonder." Much earlier, Elizabethan playwrights invited audiences to reflect on the "marvel and mystery of mere man." The psalmist of the Old Testament marveled at "how wondrously" he was made.

Dr. Ambrosino in *Date Your Wife: The Crucible of Relationship* approaches the marriage relationship from a twenty-first century perspective of this celebrated awe. He "wonders" at the complexity, dignity, beauty and richness of the human person in a faithful, dynamic relationship with another. Drawing freely from his vast clinical experience and his own broad appreciation of literature and philosophy, this very experienced therapist posits that marital happiness depends upon the ability to develop a personal security and to muster creativity that can transform familiarity into excitement and routine into ritual. He shows marriage as an evolutionary experience which, with attention, mutually enhances the relationship and enriches the individual partners. He cautions that such development is not automatic and in fact demands large shares of the best in human nature, including the moral imagination. The book reveals the author as a highly competent professional but also as an experienced practitioner of the theory he presents.

With broad but deft strokes, Dr. Ambrosino sketches the cultural forces which vitiate "awe" and diminish the illuminative and generative force required in human relationships. Woven throughout the book is the author's convincing sub-thesis that the death of marriage leads to the death of the family and ultimately to the death of civilization. He points out that the removal of boundaries and prohibitions rather than giving freedom has created a slavery of individuals and nations.

The author perceives the emergence of individual rather than universal morality, the increasing desire for instant gratification, the inability to deal with personal pain, and the "magical expectations" of life itself as lethal to human relationships and culture. Throughout the chapters, clinical examples and mini-case studies illustrate these self-defeating motivations. A skeptical reader can easily validate these by even a cursory look at the media, the displays in the neighborhood pharmacy, the long lines for the lottery and the casinos, as well as the perfectibility syndrome which fuels the weight-loss and the cosmetic surgery industries. The dread of "permanent commitment" pervades society and explains many social phenomena from the increase in co-habitation without the benefit of marriage to the decrease of vocations to religious life.

The author's analysis of human nature does not offend any faith denomination and could be helpful to the non-believer as well. His basic convictions draw on the Judeo-Christian foundational teaching of the dignity of the human person, the sacredness of the family, and commitment to the common good. Love of self and love of neighbor as oneself is central. Dr. Ambrosino's "center to center" relatedness approach challenges selfishness and self-centeredness. It incarnates the Scriptural paradox that it is "in giving that we receive" and that "in denying the self for the other" we gain new life. The very briefest reflection on the reader's part can conjure up many personal examples of how going beyond the self has not only revealed the self but has also greatly enriched it.

Secular writers would interpret this "center to center relatedness" as eschewing domination and subordination in marriage and favoring equality. Dr. Ambrosino's stress on "center" underscores not only the personal identity demanded in marriage but also the high growth potential. Expansion and extension of the self are not possible in isolated non-relational living. It is not by chance that even contemplatives and hermits have periods of human interaction built into their life-styles. Communication with our brothers and sisters, spouses and associates in an open respectful manner reveals not only who we are but who we can become.

This is where the book becomes universally valuable although it transcends the typical self-help manual. While not all persons are married, all are in relationships necessitated by career or caused by community membership. The basic cultural analysis offered and the recommendations Dr. Ambrosino suggests can be easily integrated by the single professional or the vowed religious. At the risk of distorting Dr. Ambrosino's carefully delineated diagnosis or reducing the prescription titrated to marriage, my conclusion is that any reader will find himself/herself (not only in one's present state but also in one's crucibled potentiality) on these pages.

After creating a cultural context for his professional and personal beliefs, Dr. Ambrosino first invites each reader to recognize his/her own gifted individuality from the Creator. Secondly, he quietly encourages the reader to be a good steward of those talents through effective relating and growing within the human community. In those mutually enriching encounters, whether it be within the marital relationship, the religious community or a professional organization, a healthy sense of self, a respectful stance of awe before the other will allow us to indeed enjoy life as "an epiphany of surprises" in the crucible of mutually centered relatedness.

Margaret J. Kelly, D. C., Ph.D.

EDITOR'S NOTE

The writers of the introductory matter have described eloquently the meaning and intent embedded within Doctor Ambrosino's text *Date Your Wife*.

The reader need only note a few points regarding style. While general style guidelines have been followed in the areas of spelling and grammar, Doctor Ambrosino's prose follows the sound of a unique voice. His prose style is non-clinical, yet relies upon his clinical experiences. His tone is direct, without artifice; yet, he frequently adopts a poetic rhythm. The images and metaphors encountered here are startling, even jarring because of the poetic rhythm of his prose. Style sheets and rules of prose must serve the rare and earnest tone of the author, not the other way around. His voice cannot and must not be separated from his meaning.

Jacqueline Leone

5-AMBR

AUTHOR'S PREFACE

My primary reason for writing *Date Your Wife* was to encourage husbands to become more attentive to their wives. Simply, date her! I was much surprised by their reaction to this simple recommendation. There was shocked surprise followed by a nervous laugh.

As I explored this phenomenon in writing this book, I found myself in the midst of the experience (problem?) of human interactions. Many marriages were failing and I wondered why. Also, I began to examine those marriages that lasted beyond mere adaptation. I discovered that the process of marriage was not to be an end in itself, but much more marriage had to find its rest in union, the union of spirit. Since I know more about the heterosexual dyad, the man and woman, I wrote about this pair.

By the time I had completed the book, I had realized that "wife" and "date" were generic terms which unknowingly I amplified into the implications of human relatedness. I had come to appreciate that although the religious and dyads of same-sex relationships had no wives to date, they were nevertheless confronted with the same problems of human relatedness, which sought meaningfulness. For this reason, I requested a nun, a gay person, a widow, a married couple, and a divorced person to write a preface to this book.

A wife is a wife, and is best represented in the heterosexual dyad. Important to note is that there are other people who do enter into relationships seeking and offering devotion, commitment, and love to others. In the crucible of relationship, these people also try to forge a union. Trying to understand the man and

23

woman, I went looking for a needle in a haystack and found a diamond. Indeed this adventure has been serendipitous.

In *Date Your Wife* I ask people to lift up their hearts to sacrifice for each other. I encourage that the fire within their hearts be transformed to ignite that very fire onto their hands.

Salvatore V. Ambrosino, M. D.

> "Someday after harnessing the winds, and the tides, and gravity, we shall harness for God the energies of love. And then, for the second time in the history of the world, man will have discovered fire."

-Teilhard de Chardin

ACKNOWLEDGMENTS

I want to thank my friends who were so kind, patient, and responsive in preparing *Date Your Wife*.

In publication, Patty Wolff, Jacqueline Leone, Barbara Stagnitta, Anthony Oliviero, Sandra Bordi, Andrew Mc Carthy, and John Mignosa.

For their critical review, Mike and Angela Burgio.

For the art work, Jim Pinto.

For her patience, Maria Alessi.

For her kindness, forbearance, and her insights, my wife.

"It is better therefore that two should be together, than one; for they have the advantage of their society."

-Ecclesiastes 4:9

Pen/Ink Illustration – Jim Pinto

CHAPTER I

The Workmanship of Souls

Relationships between men and women of the late 20th Century have become flimsy. If intimacy is characterized by the sharing of the core part of oneself with another, then the conjecture can be made that in its absence, relatedness has been shorn of this precious human experience, the giving of the self.

Too many of this generation live in the digital *now*. Can one imagine young people of this day having to wait for radio tubes to heat up before the radio can be *on*? It is all *now*. There is no waiting, no tomorrow: "give me now . . . don't let me wait." For them life is short. They must also have what they are entitled to. Pursuit of happiness is no longer the goal – happiness *now*. No sacrifice. Life on their terms. They ignore that joy and anguish are ineluctable handmaidens in a chancy world. In the physical world, every action has a reaction; in the psychospiritual world, every action has an emotional price to be paid. In the crucible of relationship, this *is* the ultimate reality.

Thoughts and feelings surround human beings from within and without. They are imprisoned before an unpredictable world. Behavior is the resultant of the warfare which ensues. Yet intimacy demands an appropriate exchange of embowered feelings-ideas between two people fitting very much like a lock and key, or blended like the weave of an exquisite tapestry. Intimacy demands total commitment of oneself: focused hands on the plough cannot be distracted by pleasure of the moment. Intimacy begins between two people of the *same* cloth, and cannot be bought, manufactured, or imitated. Although physical attraction is the eye opener in a relationship, the first light, the binders of relationship beyond compatibility of the surface things are values. Values are those enduring attitudes toward living things and stamp the life of a person. How a human being chooses to spend life in the brief stay on this earth looms the tapestry of his values. Intimate relationships are earmarked by decent exchanges of good will and responsive awareness.

In the golden age of psychiatry of the mid 1950's, when the human mind was accepted to be as important as the human brain, emphasis was placed on four phenomena: *transference, regression, resistance,* and *working through.* These are words that can be easily understood.

FOUR PHENOMENA

1. *Transference* refers to feelings and ideas which are displaced from one significant person to another.
2. *Regression* is an emotional retreat to another time of adaptation, or emotional strength.
3. *Resistance* is an "unconscious" avoidance of painful ideas and feelings.
4. *Working through* is a constant review of one's feelings and ideas until the distilled remnant is the truth of one's core.

Despite the birth of these four phenomena in *dynamic* psychiatry, they are most relevant in everyday exchanges. For example, the urgent need is not to confuse one person in the present with a past one. Regression can carry a hope that a present trauma may cause a throwback experience that can be used in the service of a person's growth. The acceptance that one can be "wrong" is an opportunity to listen to another. Patience to review over and over the mistakes of a relationship until a mutual honesty and harmony is reached remains crucial.

There is no doubt that two people together must put their lives into the crucible of relationship to amalgam an intimacy. Transference, regression, resistance, and working through can be used with delicacy and wisdom to bring individuals to a clearer idea of themselves. Only in this way can a man and a woman gain the freedom of self to expel demons from their human belfries and share themselves. "Mental" processes although born in clinical experience can be used as practical guides in the daily experience of making sense of relationships. Everyday do we not all *displace* our feelings like hitting a wall, and not an offending party? Do we not often deny that such behavior is part of a more immature past, and insist that others are at fault? Do not many abandon all attempts to solve *the* problem again and again?

Today the power resident in mental exploration and exchange is being displaced by the exclusive power of biology: the use of medications which promise the quickest and least expensive way to make things "normal." The importance of the paradoxical co-existence of mind and brain has shifted almost exclusively to the brain. Obsessive-compulsive disorders are now considered to be problems of the brain, and are no longer approached as a mental means to isolate painful feeling-memories. And yet in this climate in which "anything goes," we have spewed compulsive gambling, compulsive eating, compulsive drinking, compulsive sex, and soon compulsive killing. Compulsive divorce? Are these disorders of brain, or of faulty narcissistic choices – or both?

Three human experiences have taken place in the late 20th Century that seem to conspire against relationships of substance to emerge from marriages to union. These experiences are devastating to the working through of the differences that are part of *all* relationships.

The first – *feelings of shame and guilt* have been bent by rationalizations to serve individual pleasure, e.g., "I'm hurting no one," and "If it pleases me, it can't be bad."
The second – *the instant need for gratification* makes working through

impossible; self denial has been shrunken in the hands of self-satisfaction e.g., "I have no time," and "I want a cure now."
The third – *boredom* is related to people worn thin by pleasure, over-satisfaction, and magical expectation e.g., "I should be getting more in life," or "Is this all there is?"

These three experiences have minimized the importance of the other person. Many people today have not only sunk into themselves but also have now tampered with the core of their ego structure, the body image. This image is now nailed, tacked, and sucked of its substance. Just as skinny anorexics feel that they are too fat, so many today continue to tamper with the image of themselves. Pleasure-pursuit has created a crushing boredom. Many people wind up today living without hope. Their sense of being a part of a privileged human emergence is lost, and what is meaningful never emerges, because in addition, their lack of focus never defines a "precise orientation."

How can a man and woman caught up in the incessant demands of marriage survive in this new impatience of *me first*? Exclusive demands cannot be fulfilled. A marriage oriented to union cannot emerge in a marriage divided. Carnivorous needs chew up a marriage, and when these needs go unfulfilled, self-pity, blaming, and complaining take place. In this complaining, the person digs a deep hole in the sand, covers it up diligently with cardboard disguised as sand, walks back fifty feet, and proceeds to walk onto it, falls in, and screams out "who did this to me?"

If a marriage hopeful of growth requires a decent relationship of friendship, sustained by reciprocal giving, open exchange, and honest listening, how can marriage hope to grow in a setting of "I want", "I deserve", "I'm right"? Such marriages limp in continual escape into one's own pleasure with guilt and shame rationalized. In the crucible of relationship, marriage, certainly not union, cannot become a rosary of parties, restaurants, ski slopes, and Arabian nights. Dating of a special kind takes place in that crucible.

In this crucible, marriage can form that web of energy to condensate into a union, but the effort must be sustained and self-sacrificing. In the emergence of short attention spans and low frustration tolerance, this reality becomes impossible. Those unable to delay their gratifications, unable to seek some refuge within themselves, do not develop imaginative consciousness. For them, all events are concrete, pleasurable, the same, and are rarely sublimated, transformed, or delayed. Clouds can be gallows, and cows do sometimes jump over the moon. This fugitive kind never sees stars that twinkle. A world of little concern for the other, laced with weak imagination, and no affective boundaries to include others, has evolved an ethical-moral morass. In this world, human beings have lost hold of their axis of ascent and in their cynicism, they still pine for a godhead and meaningfulness.

> *Allegedly, a young high school girl, secretly pregnant, aborted her*
> *fetus spontaneously at her high school prom.*
> *She strangled the fetus and discarded it, and then returned to*
> *the dance!*

Is this an example of our human condition at this moment of our human emergence, or is this a reflection of our human nature? The former holds the hope of change from learning how to love the other. The latter is fixed. I am suggesting that when marriage remains an arrangement, it is almost sordid with no hope for growth. Marriage can be one of the avenues for a continued developmental-maturation of the human being. Just as the brain of the seventy-year-old has the capacity for further maturation, so too does marriage have that potential.

Dating is the means necessary for marriage to become a union. Dating requires a willed presence on the part of two people. Dating needs a consciousness of imagination which goes beyond mere words. Walt Whitman in his poem "A Song of the Rolling Earth" expresses this state of being so well.

A healthy presence, a friendly or commanding gesture, are
    words, sayings, meanings,
The charms that go with the mere looks of some men and
    women, are sayings and meanings also.

The workmanship of souls is by those inaudible words of
    the earth,
The masters know the earth's words and use them more
    than audible words.

The dating process is then inaudible, generous, subtle, and open handed, and cannot unfold unless there *is* a strong presence of two people.

CHAPTER II

Center to Center Relatedness

Civilization depends on order and requires a constancy of relatedness over long periods of time. Science, religion, philosophy, and art depend on such constancy. This constancy is the backbone of a particular culture such as the Indic, Sinic, Hellenic. The social cellular conveyor is the individual person who needs to be born into an organized system that fosters maturation, development, and constancy of the self. The steady progression requires time and a stable social experience. This cellular experience of constancy resides in the family, and the height of a civilization is measured by how its people are aware of each other and express themselves in their art, morality, and ethics.

Biological development and civilization depends on two *dissimilar* sexual cells, the sperm and the egg, the man and the woman. To provide stability the biological progression is guaranteed by the "rules" which became known as marriage. In this way mutual slaughter is avoided. As the major religions evolved, God was to become the key factor in the sanctification of marriage. Marriage was to ensure those ordered unions that would preserve the consciousness of a civilization, the "workmanship of souls." In our late twentieth century, the divorce rate continues to climb. One must be reminded of the following:

1. With the decline of religion, many prohibitions have been lifted, as noted in the "sexual" revolution of the latter part of the twentieth century.
2. With the extension of the life span, people have changed the quality of relatedness to sustain them not only in monogamy, but also in marriage.
3. With the change in human consciousness, the precise orientation of human beings is not exclusively directed to God in heaven, but much more to the fulfillment of their self on earth. "Sin" has taken a different meaning that has become a personal judgment.

I would like to examine marriage in the late twentieth century setting. What can sustain the human experience of a relatedness that would keep civilization secure? The emergence of drugs, suicide, crime, *is* related to the emptiness of modern human life. My theses are that family life brings a constancy of caring and belonging to each other. This caring fills in the spaces of the human soul and fosters maturation and development, and that family life is best sustained in marriage, by preserving this caring human phylum, and in turn civilization is preserved.

The questions become appropriate to ask: what has happened to marriage, and are there any solutions to this problem of disrupted human relationships? Death of marriage carries with it not only the death of the family, but also death of civilization.

A beautiful twenty-five year old woman lived with a boyfriend for one year. During the year that she lived with her boyfriend, she still managed to live a single life with her girlfriends.
In a sense, neither she nor her boyfriend had established any commitment to the relationship. When they both decided to marry, the woman began to have anxiety attacks. Her great dread was the loss of freedom and an onslaught of boredom. One month before the marriage, in an effort to experience one "last fling," she called an old boyfriend and had "sex" with him. She

felt no guilt, no shame, no sense of betrayal. No one knew. No one was hurt.

This young woman felt "fine" for her escapade. Once she began to explore the anxiety attacks, she was confronted with her dread of abandonment as her divorced mother had suffered when her father left them. The "sins" of the parents seem to be visited upon their children and leave their lives incomplete. No matter what the causes may be, carnivorous personalism and hedonism bode ill for a civilization. Relationships cannot be built upon foundations of deceit. Caring friendships are crucial for the courage to meet the unwanted surprises which life may hold for us. One way to guarantee social wholeness is through synergy.

Synergy is a working together with an orientation toward a common purpose. It is a summation of positive energies of mutual exchange and is beneficial to each. High synergy is an outstanding cooperation, such as the fingers of the hand represent in tight flexion. Low synergy is the refusal of the fingers to close. I refer to this phenomenon in human relations as *center to center* relatedness, a communion of people with no loss of self.

Center to center relatedness requires the opening of the self of its core to the other. "Love thy neighbor as thyself," or "Do unto others, as you would have them do unto you." In such circumstances, an invisible rope seems to bind the two, as is notable in the sacred union of the fetal child to its mother. This center to center relatedness creates an energy as powerful as the gravity which fills our heavens. As the invisible pull of gravity keeps things in relationship to each other, so too does the attractive power of true love penetrate the boundaries of another to become one flesh.

In O'Henry's story "The Gift of the Magi," the husband sells his watch to buy his wife a comb for Christmas. In turn, she sells her beautiful hair to buy him a watch fob. Impoverished, they draw from within themselves to give to the other, and in so doing they complete themselves. Christmas is meant to be a time for "peace on earth to men of good will." Christmas is not about getting, but is a celebration of giving. Christmas is linked to Easter, or there is no meaning to the celebration. Even in the Hebrew Seder, the warning is to be aware of the other, or else the ritual is "pure commentary."

O'Henry's story reflects the kind spirit between people of good will in which each in sacrifice is able to bring the best of oneself to the other. In the giving from the core of oneself, one brings a gift to *oneself*. This paradox brings about that center to center relatedness. The marriage of a man and woman only holds the *potential* of such a union. Much has to be worked out in the crucible of relatedness to reach the actuality of such a sublime state.

Love must emanate from one's heart, not from one's brain—least of all from one's tongue!

CHAPTER III

Love, the Hidden Substance of Faith

To flourish, marriage must become a union. Legality holds marriage in check. Spiritual enmeshing binds union. As much as financial security is important to living, relationship must be based on an individual sense of worth and a need to give of oneself. Legality is necessary when there is no trust and no real caring. From the beginning of the man-woman dyad, marriages have been geared to adaptation and survival. The needs of the husband were primary and those of the wife marginal. In a marriage that has flourished, there is union: equality, goodness, kindness, happiness, a sense of common purpose, oneness.

Women were once considered to be part of the livestock, the chattel, and indeed they were expected to carry a yoke like a beast of burden. Their dowries came to reflect their worth! In the Western World the family, the *familia*, had its beginning in the households of the Roman Empire as captive slaves. That *familia* banded together as a social unit to survive the enemy, and its needs were adaptive. Formal religions brought faith and ethics to form its foundation. As marriage has been the ordering lattice of the family, the family itself has been the basic unit for the amalgam called civilization.

In human emergence, men became associated with hunting, warfare, tool making and time; women in turn became associated with childbirth and rearing, food gathering (the first farmers?),

41

sex, and home keepers. Men were to be in charge, and women were there to be obedient passive sufferers. Men acted out; women internalized. Rare was the time when a woman was accepted as an equal friend in their arduous life. Marriage built on such a foundation cannot thrive to goodness and to the joy of completion.

Over centuries, the importance of women was split into two forms: one negative, and the other positive:

1. In a negative way, a menstruating woman was not to be allowed in wine cellars of fermenting wine. The miracle of menstruation, the life-line of life itself, was distorted into an anti-life curse!

2. In a positive way, the complete elevation of women arose in the Hebraic-Christian world when a woman, a virgin, was to bring forth the Son of God.

This attitude toward women was caught up in a marked ambivalence that civilization bore toward feminine imagination and their fecundity. Women were to have no carnal desires, and yet prostitution, even of a sacred kind, has always flourished. Mothers and wives were to be exempt. This paradox is contained in the concept of the divine harlot in which a young man looks upon his "sacred" mother as one who is without sexual needs or desires. Such a concept is part of a denial system related to the cosmic triangle of mother, father, and son.

As a derivative of this consequence, women were seen as being retaliative with their "sex." In a medieval song, Troubadour Song #50:

> *Handsome friend, charming and kind when shall I have you in my power? If only I lie beside you for an hour and embrace you lovingly – know this, that I would give almost anything to have you in my husband's place, but only under the conditions that you swear to do my bidding!*

In this song of courtly love, the woman frustrated in her relationship with her husband, seems to need some degree of control over her life, and believes her power rests in her use of sex. Or is she a nymphomaniac with no purpose in mind? Is this how women were, or did the male composer see her that way? Did troubadours of medieval times ever sing of faithful wives?

In a Neapolitan song, "Voce e Notte" (Voice at Night) there is another bent:

> *If this voice awakens you in the night,*
> *When you are holding your husband tight,*
> *Stay awake – if you wish to stay awake*
> *But pretend that you sleep deeply . . .*
> *It is the same voice when the two of us*
> *First were shyly speaking, and said 'Voi' . . .*
> *If this voice that cries in the night wakens your husband, have*
> *   no fear . . .*
> *Tell him to sleep and so reassure him.*

In the latter song, the wife is obviously unfaithful, almost openly. But once more what would prompt a woman to do this? In the former, the quest for individual control over another life as security is apparent. In the latter, there appears to be the game of marriage. What is there lacking in marriage that prompts this kind of deceit and game-playing? What effect does this have on a couple and on their children, eventually on a civilization?

Among the Eskimos, the leading cause of homicide at one time, was a wife's infidelity! In a culture that used to practice sexual hospitality, wherein the husband would choose a man for his wife's sexual favor, homicide of this kind comes as a surprise. In such cases, as an expression of her own autonomy, the Eskimo's wife most likely had the need to make her own choices. The loss of his wife's love did not bother the husband; rather, her independent choice became a mark of dishonor for him.

A man cajoled his wife into "swapping." With much reluctance, and to save her marriage, his wife agreed. Actually, she adapted to this life style better than he, but having once enjoyed an orgastic sexual experience with her husband, she slowly became numb to all sexual experiences.

In this case, one could surmise that the wife developed intense resentment against her husband who had turned her libidinal love for him into sexual performance. Sex is not love. Libido is a life force. In caring for another, the erotic aspects of sex are suffused with libido, libidinization. Sex is a function of the nervous system: the special senses of smell, vision, hearing, touch, converging upon the hypothalamus and pituitary, and down to the adrenal glands, and then to the genitals. In libidinization with its experiences of the past and present, the mind is free to express the essence of itself to another. This *is* love.

In libidinization, what was once sexual now transcends the immediate and concrete, and becomes part of all joy, without its erotic elements manifested. "Sex" dies hard and rapidly in the immediate and in repetition. Eroticism is self-love. Libidinization is extended love. In eroticism, there is a compulsive quality with few degrees of freedom, a boring sameness that forces "new" expressions; which ultimately become perverted by frustration and anger. Libidinization is like ever-returning spring – always the same, but always radiating freshness with many degrees of freedom that complete and refresh. Innovation and creativity are born in such an enlargement of the spirit. This freedom belonging to libidinization may belong to other forms of relationships such as the religious, or the homosexual pair, but at present I am discussing marriage between a man and woman as a hopeful passage to sacred union. The coming of the new "sexual" pill for male potency, Viagra, does not change this concept. If anything, this wonderful medication adds a degree of freedom to the expression of love. Used in a compulsive way for sex alone will doom it to failure. Used in tender caring will lend luster to the old wedding rings. Even the determinism of chemistry cannot expunge the need for significance and meaning.

In sex, the finiteness of time terrifies and concretizes this terror in things. In love, the finiteness of time encourages the inward journey to the self for the possibility of enduring love beyond time. This inward journey is the hidden substance of its faith.

CHAPTER IV

The Paradox Of Marriage

I shall present six marriages of a caricatured kind. Perhaps by understanding the salient, although somewhat exaggerated, features of each may bring some understanding of the destructive interactions between men and women in marriage. At the same time, some insight as to what could move a marriage to union may be gained.

In psychiatry, there are three elements to be understood:

-The *whatness*, a description of *what* a phenomenon looks like.
-The *howness*, a dynamic understanding of *how* a phenomenon comes about.
-The "*genetics*" (non-biological), the *causes* of the phenomenon.

In the marriage of *Commitment Phobia*, the man and woman play a form of "house." The experience is mainly *As If*. There are no thoughts about children, no financial plans, no burials, no shared bank accounts, no in-laws. They do have sexual lives. In a very real sense, they bear no responsibility toward each other. Everything is *now*! The outrages of ill fortune and the vicissitudes of living play little role in their planning. Their future always rests on a distant horizon, one always receding. Reality prompts it away. If pregnancy were to result, abortion would be their solution. The great contradiction is that their rationale for living together was to explore whether marriage would "work." It does not. They search for guarantees that of course do not exist. Their relationship is not bound by any pledge or vow. They mold their monuments with silly putty. Indeed there is no financial planning.

Such a "marriage" lacks a high synergy. This couple lacks the mutual cooperation of the best of themselves to create meaningful connections, such as children, extended family, and enduring homes. Adversities do not unite them, rather they separate them. They never step into the crucible to identify the hurts of the past, and never take their hurts into the service of individual growth. In most cases, this "phobic" pair have shared only "fun" and avoidance, and nurture a resistance to the understanding of their minor conflicts. When the winds blow hard in their lives, their roots are too shallow to hold them fast.

This type of "marriage" certainly holds little hope for union. Their arrangement is much more a continuation of adolescent playfulness. The setting lacks the final seal of "I am yours and together we shall build a life." Adversities that are part of life are seen as burdens, not as opportunities for working them through to growth. Their dating is geared only to their own pleasure and is never one for exchange of ideas and feelings. Even then there is no real sharing. Their dating is a constant, quiet battle against the simmering boredom of their lives. Once a surrender of the self to the other is needed, then the grand exit takes place. The fracture line of this couple is then revealed.

Indeed this couple resembles children who play "house." So caught up in their own needs, they never bring their acquaintance into relationship, and can never develop the imaginative consciousness which can bring tears of suffering to the threshold of strength, the laughter of the moment to the joy of life. For this reason the phobic couple never refine silence into an assimilation of what they have shared. They cannot bear the demands of the closeness and must therefore leap frog into activity. Ironically, they repeat the same self-satisfying charades, and wind up bored. They are moth-like when confronted with the flame of responsibility.

Their arrangement places nothing in the crucible to be distilled, nothing to be amalgamated. They are people of the *now* and nurture no vision of the future. Unable to sacrifice for another, they remain a stunted pair. They never build, but rather create ruts by running in circles. They seek a harvest of a field into which they never knelt to plant seed. The *As If* of their arrangement ends when they are bored and no longer can conjure up a sexual escapade. When the game is over, what remains is nothing. They become strangers to each other. I am reminded of Woody Allen and Diane Keaton cantering along Bleecker Street with all their bulging shopping bags, rushing into their apartment, hurriedly disrobing, getting into bed, and then looking at each other with nothing to say. Pals for a day! Love perverted. The Monopoly game is over.

> *A beautiful young woman lived with her boyfriend. She lived in dread of boredom. She often complained that the "relationship" was going nowhere. She also lived in dread of being abandoned and not being cherished. Even more, she dreaded becoming pregnant, and felt that her companion would suggest an abortion. After two years of "living together," she suffered intense anxiety attacks. She was able to see the aimlessness of her life. She finally broke free and married another. Once she found a sense of worth, she sought only people who cherished her. She learned how to give to her husband and her children. Her husband was a friend, not a pal. There were no phobic dreads of commitment. She gave of herself and no longer dreaded boredom. Her pal never did miss her, nor she him.*

In another kind of marriage wherein each partner has the opportunity to clout the other, I refer to as an *Anvil Chorus* marriage. In such marriages, the husbands are often passive-aggressive individuals. The husbands block events from happening in a stubborn, passive way. This couple harbors angry resentments, and enabling wives are the victims. They are almost never open or direct. They seem to carry an invisible guillotine, that is snapped only in their houses. Their house never becomes a home. They do not talk about their resentments. In a real way they collect injustices as a means to rationalize their withholding of their feelings. Their house becomes a vacuum.

Slowly over the years the wives fill in the gaps. These husbands unleash the marital responsibilities upon wives. In this way, the husbands occupy an unassailable seat of criticism, and are able to blame their wives for mistakes in their warfare. These husbands manage to remain popular on the job, at the "club," and are often accepted as charming by friends, and even by their children!

These husbands suffer from a "door-knobitis," for whenever they return home and turn that doorknob Mr. Hyde leaves Dr. Jekyll outside. The wives are almost never able to get others to appreciate the real situation. With this couple, there is almost never any accord – ever – from the disciplining of the children to the question of whether the seat of the commode should be kept in an upward position, or not. The condition of the house is ignored by him, and its care is left to his wife. If his wife were even to report that the automobile tires were bald, he would not pay attention to the problem!

This husband does not talk to his wife, and when he does, he grills her. He goes to work. He is not a spendthrift. He does not get drunk. He does not "womanize." And yet he never extends goodwill, nor does he ever share decent discourse with her. There is never agreement, and every decision is fraught with argument and obstruction. Never does life flow in which one moment blends into the next in a peaceful joyfulness. Neither makes the other feel good about oneself.

Usually women who marry such men think very little of themselves. Subjected to their frustrating barrage of resentment and anger, the wives become raving maniacs, or shrikes. The husbands sit back and regard them as "controlling bitches." Eventually the wife blames herself for everything. Their endless disagreements lead to dead ends: the wife screeching and the husband calmly smoking a cigarette. During her tirades, he becomes a quiet observer and looks upon his "crazy" wife. This kind of marriage becomes almost a "gaslight" experience in which the husband denies what he has done to upset his wife, and yet he has been the culprit who turned all the wall pictures upside down.

Even their sexual experiences are angry ones of blame: she is frigid, non-responsive. His penis becomes a weapon, and the exchange is masturbatory. Her enthusiasm enrages him. His wife seeks psychiatric help. She feels alone in a world crisscrossed by deceit and resentment. Not thinking too much of herself, she is aggravated by blaming herself for all that goes wrong in their lives. She is not able to reach her husband in her plight. In the psychiatrist's office, he plays dumb, and is confounded by his wife's comments. She has almost no retaliations; on the contrary, she heaps all the blame and guilt onto herself. This reversal of feelings becomes a big threat to her life.

> *A forty year old married woman was not able to get her husband to understand her unhappiness in their marriage. I first saw her in the midst of a severe depression. She was a pleasant woman who could no longer cope with her husband's complaints and obstructionistic ways. She felt useless. Finally in a gesture to emphasize her plight, she swallowed an entire bottle of phenobarbital tablets. Her husband watched her in this act. He did not call for help until she was comatose. She died.*

In the Anvil Chorus marriage, no one or anything flourishes. There is no joy of relatedness, no giving. Events pressure them together, events such as wakes and weddings. Never does anticipated joy unite them. This couple wear out and erode all feelings that once were. The husband wonders why they never speak to each other. He never confronts himself. If they go to a movie, they have nothing to discuss after the movie. They never dine – they eat with feedbags on. Their vacations are moments of pressure, and reveal how different their values and intentions are: he likes activity, she prefers walks along the shore. An amazing observation is that after divorce, what was not shared in the first marriage, the husband would share with the second – no opera with the first wife, but season tickets at the Metropolitan with the second one. The essence of this type of marriage is its unkindness and deception towards each other: she the "bitch", he the "crazy maker."

In *The Leaning Cards*, the husband is not only avoiding, but is also deeply dependent upon a very unhappy wife. He is not oppositional as the passive-aggressive husband is; much more he falls into line with any change or need without complaint or repressed resentments. The life of passive living is acceptable to him. To follow is natural for him. He is a listener without comments. He never really "hears" anything that offends him. When he dates his wife, he makes no plans, exercises no imagination, and blandly goes along with his wife. Even at dances, he enjoys his wife dancing with someone else much more than he enjoys dancing with her. His wife's pleasure is his pleasure, and for this reason he awaits her suggestions.

By default his wife becomes the leader. She becomes very unhappy in this unwanted hegemony. Her protests are all silent. There are no grinding resentments in their role reversal. Imperceptibly this transition occurs. The Leaning Cards remain faithful to each other, but the air between them is never stirred. He goes to work, and she maintains the household. His wife gradually develops a desire for someone to lift her chalice of despair, for she cannot bring herself to be openly critical of her husband. Once this wife feels unprotected and neglected, her rage becomes displaced derision: among friends, she will criticize his dress, correct his language, ridicule his eating habits, and deride his work. He accepts her retaliations without complaint.

As the wife in the Leaning Cards becomes more independent, her husband becomes much more dependent. His admiration for her grows. He brings no novelty to the marriage. He concentrates upon bringing money and things to the marriage. They buy the boat and the summer home, but there is no resonant joy in their

51

lives. His wife never develops respect for him. Deep down she feels bereft and barren, yearning for a companionship wherein there would be an exchange of the vigor and joy of shared planning for their future. She does not doubt her husband's love, and discord is not what she seeks. Without knowing it, she desires to work through their relationship in the crucible of marriage. She dreams of being Fay Wray being held safely by King Kong on the top of the Empire State Building.

Her husband is innocent, and does not recognize her suffering. Much more he luxuriates in her energy and forbearance. Their children drift. The sexual act never becomes sensual, and remains perfunctory. In fact the act is not even sexual. As with the rest of their lives, their intimate lives are shorn of passion. All becomes routine. In this type of marriage, the couples just endure. There are no tirades or rages. The roles are indeed reversed. Although the wife is eventually aware of her capability, she still seems to crave being taken care of, protected, and desired. Counterphobically, she becomes the perfect mother and wife. Headaches abound, as do fantasies of affairs. The wife in the popular book/movie *The Bridges of Madison County* is of this kind. This couple becomes lost in the routine of group experiences and raising children. The husband remains content and smokes his pipe. Their dreams once vivid die in the greenery of their financial success. What characterizes this marriage is its adaptive blandness.

When the Anvil Chorus couple dine out, the knives and forks become weapons of war. The Commitment Phobic couple never sit down to dine, they eat. In ennui, the Leaning Cards fall with their faces into their dishes.

If the marriage of the Leaning Cards was one of mutual defense against separation anxiety, and the Commitment Phobic was one of dread of loss of self, and if the Anvil Chorus couple was isolating their self-doubts from their consciousness, the *Twin Bed* marriage is one of libidinal burn out. In this experience, the couple does everything "right." They meet in the "right" place, do the "right" things. The beginning of their marriage held high promise. Their early state of being is drained by permitting others to direct their choices to fulfill an image which is held up to them. They permit others to live vicariously through them.

Indeed they are polite to each other, and often treat each other in a decent manner. What is missing however is a fire within! Passion, deep interest or caring rarely besiege their choices. They are reasonable and are in control all the time. Their clothes never seem to wrinkle. Despite the marriage's good beginning, the lack of caring connections and inner passion creates weak bonds. They are together physically, but they do not operate as a pair. Differences do exist as with all couples, but this Twin Bed group never discuss their differences. They never have a "good" fight. They never work through the ambivalence of surrender, that is necessary for all relationships to become whole. The adults of their childhood whom they have "introjected," the people whom they have "eaten," in order to preserve their being loved, exist within each of them as repressed foreign bodies. Consequently, this couple is programmed for peace, but peace never belongs to them.

This couple becomes so busy living someone else's lie that they never work through what they need for themselves. They live with one eye on the present and the other on what is expected of them. Consequently not knowing themselves, they build an invisible bridge of strangers. They lose sight of themselves in a slow way. They spend their lives sifting through the holly and tinsel of Christmas, the firecrackers of the Fourth of July, and the colored eggs of Easter. Once they are in a room alone with each other, they have nothing to say to each other, and wonder where their lives have gone. Space drowns them; time ages them. Plastic now, there is no discord, but they are still able to breathe and to eat. The experience is a democratic one, for it happens with an even hand to the wealthy, to the middle class, and to the poor. Zombies are zombies whether on the beaches of Coney Island or on the French Riviera.

Finally their plastic life of no discord cleaves the conjugal bed in twain. The proverbial brass bed becomes twins, and the ever present excuse is that the husband snores. As is their benchmark, they do not work the problem through, but seek a practical solution. They occupy separate beds. Later, separate rooms. The mornings and the nights become polite. Death rescues them with the "right" funeral. They bury strangers.

Their original hope in marriage was sculptured into one grand show filled with platitudes. Their dating at the opera or the theatre or the restaurants was never laced with those walks along the beach when they could talk about themselves. Discord meant failure. Differences meant failure. The marriage becomes a model of the Grand Picture topped by the Grand Golden Wedding Anniversary, and the count was "right" for children, grandchildren, and great-grandchildren. Their eyes were never wrinkled however by meeting the challenges of intimacy. They were never *one*, but much more a pair created by Dr. Frankenstein.

Like the Twin Bed couple, the *Perfect Couple* does everything "right." The big difference is that this couple responds to outside anthems, not those that were "eaten." This couple clamors for money and position in society. The husband may hate what he does for a living, but he earns a great deal of money. So they suffer now to buy what they want someday in the future. They postpone and gather wealth and things of no meaning. Finally, all meaningful connections are gone. The husband keeps putting off his dream to study man-o'-wars in the Palau Islands. Their honeymoon to southern France and the African safari added nothing to their connections with themselves and with each other. His wife always feels that she has failed him.

Unlike the previous couple who have one eye on the past, this couple has one eye on a future that is always receding. Once a spontaneous pair, they become rigid and circumscribed. They date, but there are no longer any exchanges of joy or wonder. They are a couple frozen in their climb on a ladder. Their lives become routine, as does their dating and sexuality. As the gold around their necks gets slowly heavier, they begin to blame each other for their emptiness. This couple fights and blames, but does not relate to the real problem. They have built their lives on a sinkhole. For an experience to be real, it must be connected to something inside the person, some value beyond the self. A dream, a hope must gush forth from the deepest core of a person. The hope to build on losses and mistakes is gone with this couple. Success to become more is vague and always a part of a fugitive future.

This Perfect Couple becomes a social mirror, but they never see themselves. The perfect house, the perfect attire, the perfect schools. He begins to drink, and her eyes begin to wander. When they move, neither wind nor dust is rustled. They raise correct behavior to a stodgy professionalism. Since they blame each other for their plight, they erect "secret" lives. Their resentments are silent, deep, and paranoid. This couple created themselves. They are a political pair who lost their compass on their way to the top. Perfect control led to nothingness, and they became impaled on pillars of gold with the Golden Fleece as a cape.

The *As If* couple are the ostriches of marriage. Their replies to questions of importance are "I don't know" or "I forgot." Often they just stare life down. They seem to melt into discord. They go through life shrugging their shoulders. This couple takes turns in playing dumb. They fluctuate between a folly of two and fabrications of the most fantastic nature. At cocktail parties, they can pair themselves off as millionaires or as Medal of Honor winners. They share and mutually support their outrageous stories.

These marriages float through life on the air of denial. With denial systems mutually shared, they become a dangerous pair, for they are able to isolate all events, and focus only on those experiences that they choose to emphasize. In this way, they are able to live in their self-made Shangri-La. Each plays his or her own part. They become a jackal pair who are able to live off others, emotionally and financially.

Even their dating and socializing are made to appear idyllic. They talk of nothing. They are empty drums that make noise. They do not lie as much as they live in a world of silly putty mannequins. Together they create their own Mad Hatter's tea party.

Trying to make sense of what they talk about, one runs the risk of developing severe headaches. They live in the essence of the As If world. Their sexual lives are a mystery, but like everything else, it is always presented as being "great." On dates or socially, they are like two glowing fireflies in August – they glow the moment and are then gone. They leave no trace. They are able to walk among the raindrops and never get wet. Their children drown. This couple moves with their heads in a smoke screen of confusion and hide the ambitiousness of the Macbethian pair. Heaven and time catch up to them.

As stated at the beginning of this chapter, these marriage vignettes are no doubt caricatures of marriage types. By presenting exaggerated salient features of each, I hope to make marital problems more accessible for study and change. No doubt there are no clear distinctions, since each bear elements of the other. In this way, we can try to discover what is corrigible. One thing is certain: for any marriage to have the hope of a union, humility and resolve of purpose are necessary. There can be no competitive right or wrong. Everyone is to be blamed, and no one is to blamed. Only then can the paradox of marriage be resolved and distilled into union.

In a paradox, the premises are acceptable and logical, but the conclusion is not acceptable. Born on a leap year, after twenty years of life, a person is not five years old! In a marriage, the thought must be that if you want to find your self, you must surrender your self!

In this modern day, the youth may attempt trial "marriage," but there can never be a trial union. This would not be a paradox. It would be a contradiction in which the part is greater than the whole.

CHAPTER V

The Harmony Of Differences

Once more, my thesis is that marriage should become a union of spirit, mind, and body. Although in union a man and woman become one, they maintain nevertheless, their individuality. Examining the six caricatured marriages, one finds that they share two common aspects:

1. A resistance to examine their past life experiences – I shall call this tendency as the *vertical* (historical) reality
2. A mutual unconscious choice to avoid entering the *horizontal* now. This vertical-horizontal complex makes up the *crucible of relationship*.

Unexamined and unshared, these six "marriages" remain stagnant and self-satisfied. What follows is the absence of spontaneity, joyfulness, commitment, and novelty. By novelty I do not mean the purchase of new things, but much more an innocent openness to find new meanings in old experiences. When they seek psychiatric help, they try to justify their own positions, and in error seek a referee in the psychiatrist. He is much more a clinical interlocutor.

An outstanding irony is that the "open" marriage in which "anything goes" is a *closed* system! As in the randomness of any closed system, such a state of affairs leads to entropy or death. In sharp contrast, a marriage that becomes a *union* is an *open* system with many degrees of freedom and choices. Freedom is not license. Marriage which does not become a union is truncated and closed-looped. A union of a man and woman is free and spiraled. The socio-psychological fallout of the former is an angry, destructive climate. With the latter, one can cross one's own boundaries to treat another as oneself. The former remains a self-involved narcissism; the latter becomes a resonant narcissism.

When people are able to clear the motes of the past from their own eyes, then will they cease to transfer their hurt feelings and ideas to the others of their present lives. As much as an individual cannot be fixated to the past, so too a couple cannot remain fixated. Even when arguments become severe, there can be no lasting regression of any kind except for those regressions in service of growth. Grudges destroy hope. People often have a glimmer of awareness of what is, even when they are distorting a reality to their own exclusive needs. These small awarenesses must be acted upon in the service of relationship.

A true union should be taken as an inviolate promissory note, a seal of vowed devotion. This seal should become a repository of appropriate expectation. The promise is so deep a commitment of faith and trust that such a promise takes on a sacred quality. One puts one's entire being in the hope that this faith and trust is being requited. The fulfillment of promises brings respect to the giver and a sense of worthiness to the other. Fullness of such a union can only spill over to bring goodness and joy for all those who come to know them in their openness. Fullness of the self can only be completed by bringing one's own humanity to another. From such a gift, only kindness and goodness can flow.

Union is marked by being there, no trials, no experiments. Union is never peripheral or tangential, but always center to center. Commitment in a true union is never conditional. The devotion of caring is always there, for better or worse. In marriage there are no guarantees. A child might be born with Down's Syndrome, or unexpected financial reverses might occur, or the death of one partner might leave a single parent. Life *is* real. Commitment costs in sacrifice, and does not survive in avoidance. Sacrifice, giving up one's comfort and one's pleasure, is the measure of true caring. When sacrifices are part of the good times, then the traumas that may follow become almost a command to assimilate the anguish in the service of the perpetuation of the love. To become a union, this is the path for a marriage to follow. In union the differences between men and women cannot then divide them. The harmony of their differences becomes the very substance of what forms an ineluctable union.

In order to shape my thesis more clearly, I must digress a bit at this point. In psychiatry, I consider the whole person, body, mind and soul, to be the Self. That part of us which experiences (analyzes) and executes action for the Self, I refer to as the Ego.

To deal with the conflicts of that world, I conceive the Ego to have outer and inner boundaries. The *outer boundaries* are made up of special senses, such as vision, hearing, smell, taste, and our position in space. In contrast, the *inner boundaries* are made of attitudes, beliefs, and ethical moral values. Expressions, "you are always in my heart," or "I love you so much that I could eat you," reflect that loved ones are taken into the Self by a process called *introjection*, and those taken in are referred to as *introjects*. To be whole, human beings must organize their perceptions, and integrate them into their experiences to create their inner world. While feelings and thoughts discharge this inner world and seek some meaningful harmony with the outside world, *temperament* shapes the final picture.

Temperament is constitutional and inherited. This inheritance is manifested in body types, and the type of nervous system a person bares. Temperament is an *habitual mode of emotional response*; nervous (anxious), cheerful (sanguine), gloomy (saturnine), stolid (phlegmatic), unhappy or irritable (dysphoric), hypercharged (hypomanic), impulsive (hyperkinetic). Temperament is not an emotion, but governs the mode of emotional response. Temperament is not psychological. Temperament is manifested in the following body types:

The endomorph – short, round, jolly type
The ectomorph – tall, slender, hungry-looking type
The mesomorph – husky, muscular, athletic type

The first has been associated with the Falstaffian type; the middle one as the Cassius type; the last, the Tarzan type.

Even the reactivity of the nervous system is inherited: from the hard-driving, hyper-focused doer to the slow moving, lay back spectator. Innerliness is that psychological-temperamental capacity to look inside oneself, and with no need to define the world by blaming others (projection). The inner self should always remain in touch with itself, knowing all the time where its toes are. This inward capacity helps to define one's own world clearly from that of another – distinct but one! When that inner connection is lost, there is disaster. More than psychological differences between a man and a woman, a temperamental misfit could be a bigger problem because attraction of the selves in harmony would require much more work. The temperamental noise, so to speak, would not facilitate the necessary inward reachings, to keep the outside world distinct and clear. With such noise the worlds to be enmeshed would be in trouble. Temperamental fit is much more than similar interests. Rather it is a governing reflection of how persons modulate their experiences.

A husband may enjoy cold weather, winter sports, and jazz while his wife may enjoy the opposite things. Such differences can be worked out between two people of cheerful disposition. The readiness to examine themselves and the desire to give one to the other and to experience another would be the key to a resolution of their differences. How they "see" the world would be the key, *viz.* agreement to cooperate is not perceived as "giving in." Once they like themselves and each other, they can recognize that these are not crucial issues, as would be their attitudes toward children, abortion, or divorce. A gloomy person is not an easy person to talk to. This is also true of irritable personalities. Personality type then is important in resolving marital problems. Respect and trust for each other remains the mainspring.

> *Once I had a patient who was depressed and paranoid. His wife was very much devoted and patient dealing with his complaints. After many months of psychiatric treatment, manifestations of neurological complications and pernicious anemia were noted. Appropriately treated, the neurological and psychiatric problems cleared up. The depression lifted. Yet his wretched treatment of his wife continued, but the marriage was sustained by his becoming a traveling salesman. His fault-finding continued.*

In this case, nothing in his personality changed that would open him up to share more of himself with his wife. This patient's brain was affected, but not his mind. His attitude did not change. He was a dysphoric personality. He never exerted himself to get to know his wife. He did not recognize that "bringing home the bacon" was not the only thing his wife needed. She needed him to share his life with her. For respect to grow, there must be a caring for the other and a willingness to share one's self. The inner boundaries must mesh, and only in this way are the temperamental differences reined in. Despite the differences between men and women, from their sexual cells to the hormones which bathe their brains, their values must be similar. The caring, the values similar, and respect in the appropriate areas foster responsibility for the other.

Although more men today are being awarded children in child custody suits, there are two biological universals which transcend all cultural changes. These universals belong to women: 1) they have a limited number of eggs, and 2) on a periodic, lunar basis, a "frustrated" fertilization leads to a hemorrhage known as their "period!" These universals put women more in tune with the finiteness of time. Biological nature puts women into a perspective which

61

has little to do with vanity or "ego." The essence of the man-woman relationship then becomes not only one of attraction, or caring, but also one of a willingness to share oneself with the other through the storms of life. They become equal partners in their passageway through life. They must share their selves, the inner boundaries. Temperamental differences become fields of force from which to grow. The dyadic matrix then becomes suffused with responsibility for each other. The husband must share his wife's vulnerability and take on the responsibility for her total being, even more so when she is with child.

The word responsibility is derived from the Latin *respondere* (to answer, to correspond). Responsibility then is a promise to be responded to, and is part of the keystone of enduring relationships. The fulfilling of responsibility requires free will and open giving. In this way, faith and trust are bred, and then there emerges a free person. Freedom is not license. Freedom *is* a human universal gift. With introjection, the "eating" of good or bad likenesses begets good or bad likenesses. The final blend or identification rests on the faith in the relationship and the choices made.

> My grandson Michael at five years old was getting accustomed to jumping into the pool. Before jumping in with his arms outstretched, he would look me straight in the eye and I would keep repeating, "Ok Mike, jump, jump, grandpa is here," and he would jump. Each fulfillment of his trust created a strong bond of his faith and trust in me.

Acceptance of responsibility and trust go hand in hand, and it is also an expression of freedom on the part of the giver, as well as the one who chooses to receive. Such a partnership in effort is the keystone to marriage.

During pregnancy women undergo transformations. They accept to put their bodies through a veritable torture of pain, deprivation, sacrifice, and danger. They put their own needs to one side in order to bring forth a living being, once center to center physiologically, always center to center psychologically and spiritually. By their free choice and caring trust, they transform the frightening spectre of childbirth into one of creation and hope. The pain is forgotten. This deep down sharing and caring is the foothill of intimacy so crucial to transform marriage into union. Strangely, the mother and infant need no weaning of inner boundaries; their intimacy just *is*. And in this way, once the husband becomes a true partner in the creation of relationship, marriage alters its course to the greater complexity of spirit, Union!

I have used the word intimacy a number of times. It is a word derived from the Latin *intimus*, the innermost! The essence of intimacy is sharing the innermost part of the self with another. This sharing is a daunting task. To give of oneself is not an easy matter, for human beings tend to give only when they can get. Their *vertical* reality must be swept clean from the "I want" and the constant flight into self gratification. Intimacy is in part learned from example. Unfortunately, to be intimate has come to mean "to have sex."

For a marriage to develop and mature into a true union, there must be not only the intimacy of values, but also a vision for the future. Intimacy and vision flourish only in the climate of trust. Perfection in marriage should not be sought. Much more, sincerity, honesty, and deep caring should be the goals. Unfortunately, with deep caring there come five dreads that can discourage many people to love:

1. Loss of self
2. Loss to death
3. Unrequited love
4. Humiliation with loss of self-esteem
5. Annihilation of the self by flooding feelings.

Loss of self: In having intercourse with his wife, after having solved some basic conflicts, a husband began to experience loss of feelings in his penis. His wife had become very close to him, and part of her deep responsiveness produced increased vaginal lubrication. He then complained that he had lost the center of himself and became impotent.

Loss to death: A married woman was an artistic performer. At times her troupe would travel. During these moments, she would miss her husband a great deal. She began to associate these separations with death. The dread of his death would leave her emotionally paralyzed. Her solution to such putative loss was to "pick up" a stranger, on the night before returning home and have "sex" with him. She tried to dilute the "loss," the hurt, and tried to gain a reassurance that she could live without him.

Unrequited love: A patient had a great fear of not being loved as he loved. He would therefore get women to the point of their desire for a deeper commitment. At that point he would withdraw immediately, or he would invite them to live with him. Satisfied that they wanted the security which he represented and not him, he would then cut off. He dreaded that he would love someone, and they would want "his money," not loving him at all. So he exposed himself to what he feared.

Humiliation: A husband complained of his wife's sexual frigidity. Solving some problems in therapy, his wife became much more receptive and responsive to him. She was no longer a "mummy", and her husband was stunned. He felt vulnerable, and concluded that if his wife could perform that way with him, she could respond in like manner to other men. He became impotent because he felt that his wife's behavior humiliated him.

Annihilation of the self: In her first sexual contact with a man, a young woman's orgastic reaction was so intense that her

*self "dissolved." She adopted a homosexual lifestyle thereaf-
ter in an effort to regain her self.*

These five "dreads" seem to bear in common a "secret self"
which is exposed by the dread of loss. These fearful people have
lost the connection between their *vertical* past and the *horizontal*
experience of *now*. These people of dread carry such a poor sense of
self that the smallest sharing threatens them. They live with their
necks resting between the flying blades of the scissors of time.
They lack not only permanence, but also they never find the center of themselves. They cling to life and wrap themselves in ac-
quired things, fun, and gossipy turmoil. There is no music of hope
in their lives, and for them the earth becomes a "valley of tears."

Like all living things, we are in a constant state of unfolding or
becoming. Human beings cannot walk until the long nerve fibers
of their nervous systems become surrounded with myelin, a fatty
tissue. Maturation and development are crucial to human emergence, but this unfolding must take place in a propitious environ-
ment. And so it is with marriage. Being is an interpersonal experience, and marriage must therefore mature its potential of love into
the actuality of union.

The "dreads" indicate that human beings are aware of time,
and are able to reflect upon their futures. Dreads that become
compulsive seem to be a refusal to pay the price that the paradox
of life imposes: everyday life brings one closer to "the inevitable"
hour of biological death. Even the Catholic prayer, the Hail Mary
ends with "pray for us sinners, now and at the hour of our death."
Human beings carry this awareness of vulnerability every day of
their lives. Compulsive routines of denial neither sweep the tides
back into the ocean, nor do they cause grains of sand to jump back
up into the hour-glass. Biological time is not reversible; it is a one
way street. How does then one stay real in a marriage in the midst
of such a dilemma, a searing paradox?

The dreads must be confronted as opportunities to work
through the developmental kinks. Life must be taken as an

epiphany of surprises. Maturity in life must be measured by calculated risk taking, and spontaneity as the measure of normalcy. Spontaneity comes from within the free self, and although it is joyous, it is never self satisfying. In the crucible of relationship, one distills free the psychic splinters of the excess baggage that people gather in life. Human beings live on a blue speck surrounded by a vast, incomprehensible universe. All they have is each other. The dread of aloneness without shared memories of love and loved ones is not much better borne than by the loneliness of just memories without shared love. Recently on a beautiful day, I went to Coney Island. I passed the old *Thunderbolt* roller coaster of my childhood. On that day, I remembered the happy memories of my childhood with my parents and sisters near that very roller coaster. It has now been abandoned, but a beautiful trumpet vine has coiled its rusting skeleton. At first there was a deep painful pang in my heart, but once I remembered the loving memories of my parents and my sisters and those innocent days, I smiled and blessed the roller coaster of my childhood. She just stood and waited, but she still served.

Conquering these dreads for the sake of love gives marriage the possibility for self-perfection and self-differentiation. Marriage certainly demands that one must go beyond the self. Marriage in development does not blur individual boundaries. Much more, it defines them. These dreads cannot be resolved by mere *role playing*. In his autobiography, Mortimer Adler, the great Thomistic philosopher, replied that he did not become a Catholic although their dogmas were "viewed as comprehensible, as reasonable, and as believable." Quoting Acquinas, he called this situation "dead faith" in contrast to "living faith." Living faith required charity, the love of God, and the *will* to live in accordance with that love. To deal with the dreads of loving perishable beings requires love that is a *living* love and a *living* faith.

Role playing is a conscious effort to have things work. Marriage is much more than making things work. Role playing is destructive because masks are worn to direct the other to one's own exclusive needs. In role playing, there is not even the intention of the common good, but much more the need for selfish fulfillment. Caution must be exerted in drawing conclusions on this matter. A man can be as nurturing as a woman can be assertive. Neither may be role playing. Each may be expressing definite feelings of an inner experience about what they care for and what they actually feel.

> A wife felt increasingly isolated from her husband. She told her husband. His solution was one of a game: he would call his wife during the day and "interrupt" her sexual encounters with the delivery man or the postman. This was all fantasy. During their actual sexual experiences, his wife would describe the details of what "happened." At one point of the "game," having gone to the tailor shop, she actually did permit herself to be seduced. Later she had incorporated this experience into their "game." It was not until a vacation to the Caribbean that her husband, after returning to their room from a swim without her, found her sprawled on the bed, nude and asleep. He awakened her. She told him that the chamber maid had seduced her, and that she "loved it." Indeed it happened, but her husband no longer could tell what was real or fantasy.

In a marriage that is to grow, the tracks are not parallel, for there is but one track. The whole intentionality is geared to a shared synergistic future. No time is spent on games, or role playing. The growth of the marriage requires all the energy that one can muster, and this energy springs from deep within the self. As the earth pores its stored energy into the stalks of our vegetation, so too must the energy of marriage gush forth from within. The devotion, the caring for, the nurturing must come from the deep self and is never stylized by role playing. The spontaneous desire of one to fulfill the need-want of the other lifts the relationship out of a dead marriage into a *living* one, for it is now *love* with a willingness to sacrifice and a will to keep the awareness of the other always in mind. A living marriage is not self serving.

Having a role however is not role playing. A role defines boundaries that have biological roots as well as psycho-social roots. The psychic manifestations can find men tender and women assertive. The vision is almost paradoxical that a woman who would stand by her husband's side during enemy attack would also have a need to be helped up to their covered wagon. A historical figure who exemplified these traits was Abigail Adams. In a living marriage, *Caritas* suffuses its substance and sets up a resonance of exchange.

The union which marriage must become to have meaning cannot solely be utilitarian. Practical use of each other is only part of the marital process. Needs must be distinguished from wants. The former are crucial to the center of the self, whilst the latter are part of the process. Marriage with a precise orientation toward union has to do with meaning, and for this reason, sacrifice and values are its benchmarks. There are no tricks or sleights of hand. In marriage, the elements of roles are tacitly and appropriately exchanged. By values in marriage, I mean that a man and woman must assign worth to different aspects of living in consensual agreement. These aspects concern human behavior and concerns, as well as how one's attitude towards life affects the other. One must often give what one cannot afford to give. To give a prized comb means much more than giving a bar of gold which has little value for a person. The comb could be worth one dollar, but could have belonged to one's mother. On a whim, a millionaire could have given gold of no meaning to him. A prized linking object such as the comb ceases to be a mere material object. Invested with feelings the object becomes one of ultimate concern and a link to the heart of another.

True giving is unafraid of risk. True giving is spontaneous. True giving is responsible. True giving is open and resonant. True giving springs from the inner core of the feeling self. True giving links precious people. True giving requires a freedom which only a lucid mind can yield. True giving is the essence of marriage to become a union.

As mentioned before, human freedom rests on vertical and horizontal roots. Once more vertical in that the feeling-behavior stems from the *past* when the young mind was impressionable, mimetic, and dependent for survival. In the need for survival, the young mind adopts the ways of others. In this adaptation, other people enter their minds as introjects through the Should-Should Not system of the superego, the social conscience. This desperate introjection, or "eating" of people, carries with it a repressed modicum of resentment. The push-pull of this experience renders the experience ambivalent - "I love because I have to" and "I hate you for my loss of self." In a festering ambivalence, these introjects become "psychic splinters" and rob the individual of choices. Only the working through of the ambivalence creates the climate of freedom. When those early caretakers in charge of young people give of themselves, not for themselves, and do not live their lives through entrusted young minds, the vertical experience becomes a resonant narcissism. These early caretakers are then assimilated into the warp and woof of identification.

The vertical dimension is a developmental one, and is therefore subject to retreats (regression) and fixations (freezing of the ego). A frightened, narcissistic caretaker becomes a foreign body, "a splinter" in a young conscience structure, and robs the young mind of the experience of failure and the asking of good questions. Such imprisoned minds are frozen to what "they" think or say, and in this absence of a lucid mind, there can be no freedom, and consequently no true giving. Their marriages become nightmares of misdirections and accumulation of things. They do not know how to be honest and never can become whole. Their intentions are always split.

A young married man had trouble dealing with marital pressures. He could not deal with arguments, and therefore he could not resolve differences with his wife. For some reason, he always resented how easy it was for his father to listen and to deal with disagreements, especially with his mother. In difficult situations, his father always had a cup of coffee and an open mind. In therapy, the patient did work through the source of this jealousy and his dread of loss of himself. His discussions ceased to be power struggles, and he was then able to define his own ideas about life. He loved and admired his father. To behave with openness and understanding was not a submission, but a judgment to use a better way to solve problems.

The flow of the past into the present can render to a person freedom so crucial to giving of oneself. Disagreements in marriage are much more readily resolved by being able to speak over long cups of coffee, rather than in the silent, grunting of the sexual bed. The horizontal *now* as mentioned is rooted in *immediate* affective happenings. In the clear choices of the present, human beings can walk a clear road. When psyches have been bogged down by the "foreign" bodies, they walk about as if in a fog, and repeatedly make choices in which they "shoot" themselves in the foot. Those with clouded expectations of marriage, those still fixated in the nostalgia of the past, those who have never differentiated themselves to remember whether it was strawberry or vanilla ice cream which they preferred, go about as if they are blind in a slaughterhouse. Horizontal affective realities are pressing and imperative, and are markedly fueled by the past.

Traumas of the *now* can be used in the service of growth. Marriages are not then doomed by individual history. While a person is alive, hope is always alive. A deep desire to be whole must steer feelings, ideas, and behavior all in a precise orientation to a life of meaningful connections. Free access of the horizontal experiences to the vertical possibilities renders marriage an open system.

A young woman was ready to be married. She did not heed her mother's warnings that the man she was to marry was a psychopath. No logic could alter her course. She felt that her mother was a failure, and her advice useless. Most of all she felt abandoned by her father. I had known the patient as a child. As the years passed on, she would call me in desperation for an appointment, one day before my vacation. Her relationship with me was replete with "I don't know" and crying copious cataracts. For some strange reason, her husband to be displayed open expressions of wanting to control her, often with cruelty. At last her self esteem offended, she connected up her intense anger with her father, for treating her as if she were of no value to him. She broke the engagement.

What renders these vertical-horizontal connections dynamic are their growth potential. Marriage is not a flatland world, but much more one of great potential. In the last example, the young woman made the connection that the caring protection which she had craved from her father became misdirected to a sadistic psychopath who spoke with a forked, silver tongue. And from him she had accepted fool's gold.

For marriage to become a true union, two people must be *free* to make responsible decisions and to learn from mistakes. The archaic past exists for each partner. Together with a precise orientation to the future, their past can become an avenue for growth. Marriage to become a union does not respond to excessive displays of adolescent love, but does require the open dynamics of the past and the now. The working through produces that lucid mind so crucial for true morality and true giving. In marriage, there can be no hiding in the circumstances of finances, jobs, professions, parents, and failures. These circumstances are always hidden opportunities with which to enter the crucible of relationship.

Differences in temperament, constitutional though they may be, can be dealt with by people of good will, open conversation, and affection. Sojourns into that crucible produce friendship. True friendship can direct temperamental differences with the seamless realities of imaginative consciousness. The incompatibility of branches may still lay down roots as interwoven as those of redwood trees. A real marriage is not made up of the clear swings of the ideal, but is always somewhat off-beat to sustain the swing as with a pendulum.

Dating holds the opportunity for imaginative consciousness and lends the necessary off-beat opportunities in which a marriage may grow.

CHAPTER VI

Dating: The Evidence Of Things Not Seen

When human beings are considered to be real, then they possess feelings, thoughts, and dreams which are appropriate to each other. The binding force of the individual is the ongoing force of life to attract and to incorporate the outside world. This is called *libido*. This incorporation not only completes the self, but recreates itself. This attraction-assimilation is the basis of enduring cultures and abiding relationships as noted in marriage.

Appetite is the driving force for completion, as with hunger toward food and sex toward the relief of tension, detumescence. Appetite is hunger at one time, and desire at another. Appetite is the psycho-physiological pathway for libido. Appetite gains the foothold for human beings to empty themselves of narcissistic, physiological swellings. In marriage, sex is the vehicle for life, but for life to live and to breathe, a life force or libido must bring a person beyond the self. Once a child is born to *living* people, the child takes on an importance beyond the sexual cells. Libido then uncoils marriage beyond self-satisfaction and self-indulgence that others become more than the self.

For a marriage not to cave in on itself, the relatedness between the man and woman must extend beyond their own needs. This is how union begins. Only in such beginnings do men and women embark upon perfecting each other. This kind of giving contains

73

that transforming factor which takes the substance of entropy or death into the grace and hope of *meaningful* connections. Sex alone can never achieve this human experience. As human beings mature, sex lingers on as a quiet need to unite oneself to another. In a marriage with children, this quiet need sensitizes one to the other in a completing fashion.

Idealistic as this may sound, if marriage is to survive, this type of marriage-union must take place, especially since life expectancy approaches one hundred years. Marriage between "objects" cannot survive, only two in one flesh and spirit can. The choices in our society are so many, so distracting, so material that the focus of marriage can easily be lost. The best way to maintain this focus for libidinal maturation is dating.

Dating is the crucial part of the maturation of the marital relationship to foster intimacy. As noted, intimacy is center to center relatedness. Dating should be a repeated attempt to recapture the mystery and the exciting promise of the first meetings. In early dating, there is a strong desire to please and to be attached to. In early dating, each brings the best of oneself to the other. In early dating, couples talk, dream, and plan. Along the way of life, sad to say, something is lost.

What destroys the early passion of dating? Passion is not sexual desire. Passion is not heated up feelings. Passion is not a function of the sexual organs. Passion is the feeling-state of being in which a person seeks a connection or a completion with another. Fear does not destroy passion. The feeling state of passion is pristine and is never diminished by the anguish which abounds in life. Passion dies in self-satisfaction and in the boredom of *expected* entertainment. Soul mates never die. They never divorce. Soul mates form a union. Soul mates are an indissoluble pair. A soul mate can be understood in two ways:

1. The first is descriptive when each draws the lines of one's limits, i.e., what they can give, and what they expect of others – this is "drawing the line in the sand" concept.

2. The second is based on being (ontological). If one entered into heaven, and God said that heaven had been earned and offered only one person with whom to be on a magic carpet forever, that person chosen would be a soul mate.

A soul mate is not a playmate. A soul mate knows the inner self of the other and is never thwarted by human foibles. For reasons that she understood and accepted, Abigail Adams had to bear long absences from John, and although "smitten" by Jefferson, John remained her innermost friend and husband.

Dating is a time to come out of the haze of the hustle and bustle of everyday life. A day does not go by that human hearts are not burdened by events that can be seen as threatening to their lives. A day does not go by that these very hearts would like to unburden their loads. Conversation is such a medium for unburdening, and conversation with its ventilation is the vehicle for dating. Not golf, nor tennis, or sailing in themselves, but much more what goes on between two people is the important ingredient. Motoric experiences only take on meaning when they are occasions to share feelings with another. This sharing is not a clinical psychiatric nightmare, but much more it is simple heart to heart talk. Dating does not require the dance floor or the opera. Dating does not need a place. Dating can just be now! Simply, dating requires undivided attention, good will, responsiveness, and a wanting to be there - and "there" can be anyplace.

The final scene, in the movie "As Good As It Gets," when the much older hero wants to express himself, his "dating" is spontaneous, and takes place at four o'clock in the morning. He convinces the heroine to go with him to buy hot buns. And it is then he tells her how good she makes him feel about himself. In the final scene, he walks on the cracks of the bricks, and they enter the bakery together.

Soul mates are linked by small things, but they do need periodic connections that dating affords. Lives can become cluttered with small, inconsequential things that people may magnify, and in doing so they may ignore what matters.

> *A husband liked green peppers, but his wife consistently bought red peppers. No matter what he said, or she said, they both unsaid what the other had said. He never got green peppers.*

This mis-buying was not a small matter, and it was not about peppers. Much more, caring and being cared for were the issues. If a marriage is to grow, one must listen with a "third ear." In such cases as the wrong peppers chosen, the key problem was that the husband and wife never confronted themselves with their real problem: the early attractions were mainly physical. Neither realized that as relationships move on, demands for intimacy become more imperative.

Mistakes are splendid opportunities to work out differences and misunderstandings that are part of all close relationships. Indeed life is full of errors and missteps, and although overcoming them wins no one a Nobel Prize, these small achievements put one in phase with the pulse of life. Battering self-defeat is self-generating, but honest failures are open to any desire to grow. Without doubt, small achievements must be shared in marriage, for in doing so one brings closure to developmental problems. Only in this way is a springboard provided for greater personal growth. Only in this way is there a more secure melding of the relationship, a greater hope for the marriage to become a union.

> *A divorced woman was upset because she had to admit to herself that she permitted people to abuse her. One day she had gone shopping and noted that the salesperson had not treated her properly. Out of character, my patient reported the incident to the manager. The issue was settled to her satisfaction. She had an excited need to share this new experience with her husband. Her husband had been too tired to listen. Crushed, she never brought*

her new experiences to her husband. Thereafter, she sought out her
girlfriend who "was always there for me."

Inattention and lack of sensitivity to the needs of the other create deep resentments that often become repressed. They take on strange forms in everyday living, such as complaining about her husband's shirt, his hair, his sexual responsiveness. Chronic discontent and irritability follow. In the above example, the wife not only closed off to protect herself, but did so completely that she began to think that she was a lesbian. Her resentments toward her father had also been buried a long time – "he was too busy making money, and was never in on what was happening to us." Her husband's reaction of non-concern over her grand achievement triggered off past resentments of similar behaviors that only reinforced her present resentment. Her reinforced frustration with her husband cut deeply into her feminine need to nurture and surrender herself in love. Her marriage eventually wove a pattern of withholding, deception, and betrayal. Spontaneous conversation was lost. The marriage lost the opportunity to rise to the higher level of union.

Establishing a more "perfect" relatedness in marriage takes more than time. Things certainly do happen in time, but corrections must take place in time. Marriage like life should be an unfolding. Life should be more than changed behavior. In any good relationship, especially in marriage, there must be much more a feeling-understanding. Hope must surround a good marriage. Human beings are flesh and blood who seem doomed to have to perfect themselves beyond their own needs if they are to become whole. For a human being to permit another person entrance into one's body and soul is a frightful act and demands much courage, good will, and faith. And "faith is the substance of things hoped for, the evidence of things not seen" (Whitman).

Dating is a time out, a pause. By common consent, each in a marriage puts all cares, fears, and woes to one side to bring the other inside the self. Such a common need seems to be an uncommon experience. When such an experience *is* experienced, private as it may be, how public the impact is! Conversation and ventilation are the vehicles of dating. Dating does not require a special place. Dating does not require a romantic setting or a special activity. Dating can take place over a cup of coffee, or walking along the beach. The key element is that each wants to be with the other, not just to have and hold, but to listen to and to understand despite the opinions of the other. The awareness must be held indelible that there are *always* distortions in any relationship, especially in marriage. The crucible is structured by open and caring concern latticed by trust. As noted, small, urgent matters can roost within one's breast for a long time and can suck the fiber of a relationship dry. Dating offers the opportunity to climb into that crucible with the distortions. For this reason, dating offers a married pair the opportunity to seal meaningful connections. In this crucible, relationships become uncluttered. Graciousness and kindness must surface to open the hearts of people. Life is much more than daily bread, more than adaptation. Chicken soup given with a full heart is transformed into something much more than chicken soup. And so it is with marriage.

Once more to become a union, a marriage must be *transformed* by sacrifice, devotion, and caring. The destructiveness of carnivorous egoism is sustained in the need for vengeance and self-righteousness. To progress from that misery to the joy of hopeful marriage requires the transforming power of selflessness. The "happily ever after" of the storybooks is the ending for a fantasy, but only the beginning for a hopeful marriage. To be remembered again is that a pendulum clock to sustain a harmonious swing must be somewhat offbeat in its mechanism. In the same way, the imperfections inherent in close sharing, once dealt with, sustain the marriage, and provide for the passageway to the harmony of union. Our archaic, unsolved pasts, and the imperatives of the *now* cannot help but bring excess baggage to the portal of marriage. In this era of expanding consciousness and myriad choices, in this time of "anything goes," marriage and its destiny to union is under serious siege.

For this marital transformation, emotional growth is necessary. What one feels, thinks, and how one acts must *all* go in one direction. They must be consistent and appropriate. Distorted emotional developments settle in "bad" marriages with the wrong partner. The characteristic of the "bad" marriage is that the couple play "roles." As discussed, role playing is the pouring of cement between two people: a wall, fixed and linear, with no dynamic imperatives for role differentiation and no opportunity to transform errors into hope. Role playing is a covering up to perpetuate the past. The frozen past robs the hope of transformation, and narcissistic arrogance nails it to a dead cross with no horizon for the future.

> *A husband would become angry with his wife whenever she ate with gusto, or was sexually responsive to him. All this he felt was a sign of her weakness and excess. Actually, his response was a derivative of how readily his mother shared her friendship with people. She was a woman of passionate involvements. In his youth, he suffered all this, and he blamed his father for permitting this behavior. This "vertical" experience colored all his life, and he repressed its origins. He had eroticized his mother's passion, and unable to stop her behavior, he transferred the problem to his wife. This past fixation had to be undone and it was.*

In this last case, the husband no longer experienced his wife as a challenge. One of the big changes was a small step. After going to the movies or to the opera, he would stop at a coffee shop and speak to his wife about her reactions to what they had heard and seen.

CHAPTER VII

The Opportunities Of Dating

Dating is not a mere opportunity for getting away from it all, "fun." Dating is not an opportunity to escape boredom, marital routine, or the pounding headaches from the demands of children. "Fun" must be appropriate, but fun does not deliver the essentials of what holds together a *particular* relationship such as marriage. No doubt getting away from it all *is* crucial at times in order to recharge oneself, but there are appropriate ways to achieve this renewal. Dating supplies these ways.

While boredom is a normal part of life, its effect can be mitigated by people remaining close to whom they are, by giving to others, and by bringing imagination into one's life. Routine is part of the necessary basic structure upon which imagination must return, or else chaos could never return to order. The boundaries of the self needs limits. The heart and its diastole and the nervous system with its refractory periods are creative rest periods.

While dating itself will not solve the problems of marriage, dating lends opportunities for married people to listen, to learn, and to correct what damage has been done to the intimacy of their relationship. Dating between a husband and wife can be fulfilling and joyful.

Dating presents opportunities for:

1. **Giving,**
2. **Reacquaintance** with the small past experiences which were once cherished,
3. **Rediscovery** of what new growth has taken place, and
4. **Libidinal Transformation**

These opportunities cannot be fulfilled only in moments of "romance." Over the rainbow nostalgia will not nurture the roots of these opportunities. Good intentions are not enough. Past mistakes cannot be rectified by repeated empty pleadings for forgiveness. Spoken expressions of love and easily sworn vows do not nurture intimacy. The stern demands of a true union need another kind of trumpet, for the sounds must come from deep within a person's soul, from within their very being and longings. Compatible temperaments make the problem easier but, with love and respect two incompatible personalities can bridge the egotistical gaps.

> *If one member of marriage voted Democratic and the other Republican, this would not necessarily be an issue. However, if the differences concerned matters such as divorce or abortion, matters crucial to their deeper sensibilities, then each would have to be able to listen carefully to the other. The resolution of temperamental differences requires much respect and trust. The foundation of a union is concerned with matters of life, survival, and ethical-moral concerns of the other.*

As defined before, inner ego boundaries are made up of feelings, ideas, and attitudes about life and living it. For a union to take place, these inner ego boundaries must be harmonious with those of the other. The essence of union *is* characterized by a deep sharing of similar values. An openness of spirit and mind follow. If this give and take occurs before marriage, the deep differences could be noted and rectified. Then the differences manifested during the marriage are able to be worked out. When two people care for each

81

other and see the opportunity to give to the other, the problems of marriage can be worked out. Giving can take place in open understanding and exchange.

When people are haunted by shadows of over-idealization of their own bodies, their parents, and themselves, they cannot be open to any world other than their own. Such people are frozen and are not able to look beyond their own needs. Marriage requires exchange. Marriage cannot become an escape hatch into a psychotherapeutic encounter, and certainly it is not a battleground for the sexes. In marriage, there is that unique opportunity to give and to perfect a shared life. In marriage, the mourning for the past idealizations must be put to rest, and the shadows of the past put away. The past becomes then a reference point, not a hitching post. The union begins when the battles end.

> *A fifty-six year old man left his wife of thirty-five years. He did this suddenly and for no obvious reason. He had a thriving business and a loving family. What had been revealed later was that he had an enlarged prostate (BPH). The enlargement was treated surgically (TURP). He had difficulty in accepting that he had retrograde ejaculation, or in his own words, "I'm shooting blanks." He never spoke of this problem. His wife accepted this "side effect." He ran away because he felt sterile, "old" without sexual power. We found him living in the Midwest. His sons got him to return back home, and his understanding wife opened herself completely to him.*

Simple talking did not dispel the shadows from this marriage. What did help the marriage was that his wife unconditionally accepted him. Giving must be open, and requires unguarded listening. Dating is an ideal time for this giving to take place. To listen to the small things and to convey understanding is crucial. A nodding awareness conveys the idea that one is listening and understanding.

The here and now is important, but experiences must be connected to the core of the self. This is not a simple matter. To bring someone into the private regency of the self requires shared faith and trust. When there is real caring, there is much less need to be "right" with private agendas, and much more a need to share one's inner feelings. Life can only be transformed from death and error by selfless giving.

The opportunity for giving must take place in an atmosphere of spontaneity. Ghosts of the past, those shadows which hover in human minds, must not foster nostalgia to past fixations. Giving, prompted by a need to give to another, not only brings hope to another, but also in turn defines the self. Dating of the real kind offers that opportunity to give. Innovation and novelty are its keynotes. There is no room for role playing. Well honed intuitions often lie dormant within many, and tacit insights should be nurtured in dating.

Although there are always daily routines to fulfill in any relationship, such as bills to be paid, obligations to be fulfilled, promises to be kept, the richness of the relationship must always be nurtured. Special time must be reserved for one another: a short walk together, a cup of coffee, a stroll along the beach. Small gestures are necessary to feed "the inner man" and "the inner woman." This cannot be an exercise, but much more a deep down burning need to sustain what once was, or else to resurrect what too soon died.

A good date is marked by the opportunity seized to give spontaneously to a kindred soul. The awareness must be sustained that what was once vibrant can be drowned in the noise of the commerce of the day. Expectations should not be taken as demands, but as needs to be fulfilled to keep the relationship alive. The expectations should be realistic. A woman who lost her leg cannot very readily go skiing! For marriage to become a union the dating must be resilient in giving, and its possibilities must be explored with imagination:

> *Intuitions* as hunches
> *Contemplations* as remembrances understood

Caring feelings as "you make me feel good about myself and
I must bring the feeling back to you,"
Expanded awareness as "living for myself is misery."

The idea of caring and giving is not an abstraction. The situation is one of real feelings and real choices. These ideas of giving require mutual trust, respect, and open honesty. When a demand is extravagant, two friends will know. The wife without the leg may know how important her husband's climb may be, and although unable to go with him, she can help prepare the trip. In the same way, her husband could modify the climb, and find another mountain, another path. The willingness to walk through life with all its hopes and anguish must be embraced as the *deal* accepted in order to become human. In dating, a man and woman must prepare to give to each other, beyond mending fences. They must have a fervent desire for reacquaintance, and thereby rediscovery to move more from the triangle of childhood and the dizzying circle of adolescence to the spiral of maturity.

A long lasting relationship is not a chronic condition. A chronic condition smacks much more of tedium, circular routine, and predictability, with little hope for change. In such a state, time is flat and blunted. Chronic implies dull habit with no hope for transformation. In contrast, enduring relationships have meaningful connections. The inescapable routines ironically free the moment from the present distractions for the next connection. These progressions of stop-go sustain relationships to remain open and fresh. Red lights and green lights are necessary at intersections to guarantee a smooth flow of traffic. Lasting relationships are not self-seeking. They always have the potential for more choices of novelty and clarified feelings.

For a relationship to become long lasting, renewals are necessary, hopefully of a much more experienced kind. Fool's gold is separated from true gold. Renewals become then reacquaintences with past experiences with the dross removed. At each new re-experience there is a new spring board from which to experience

new enlightenments. Dating offers that opportunity to renew relationships, to reacquaint the couple with the best of what is and
what was. Sometimes, one must go back to the beginnings of a
relationship to find the best of what once was hoped for. To re-
experience past feelings of what was the best.

Dating indeed offers that opportunity to renew relationships,
that opportunity to go back to the beginning to find what was
lost. To re-experience past feelings of goodness and tenderness and
hope is crucial for the growth of a relationship. For a renewal to
take place distractions must be eliminated. The past successes must
be kept in mind, and these memories will provide pause to re-
experience that intimacy and good will once known. Life, and certainly marriage, can pile up distortions, and yet a little success
with caring for another and the awareness of how brief life is can
move people to change.

> *A long married couple got bogged down in the little things of*
> *everyday living: which end of the tooth paste to squeeze; should*
> *the commode seat be up or down; the frequency of intercourse.*
> *His wife had become caught up with the grandchildren, shop-*
> *ping and taking care of her old parents, while he was taken*
> *with the routine of commuting to work, taxes, the budget, and*
> *"getting older." They stopped speaking to each other, and their*
> *communications, when they occurred, were irascible, cynical,*
> *and fault finding. Yet they still loved each other. Once asked*
> *about their first date, they both smiled. They remembered the*
> *boardwalk at Coney Island, the penny arcade, the roller coaster,*
> *the hot dogs. Like with a favorite song, they were brought back*
> *and remembered what they once had. The peccadilloes of life had*
> *worn them down.*

This couple later went back to Coney Island and while the
return of the natives did not "cure" them, they touched the home
base of their souls. The early memories and renewal of their past
joys swept away the blizzard of noise which had become part of

their everyday "modern" life. Once real love, real caring, is part of life, there is *always* hope of reacquaintance.

Like great music, a relationship is always seeking its home key. This couple revisited the foundation of their friendship through dating. As in the beginning, they tried to please each other. In a renewable experience, the past errors are corrected, and expectations are refitted to a more realistic world in which marriage can grow. Redesigning one's expectations is certainly not a sign of failure, but much more, a sign of maturity - the willingness to face one's self.

> *A forty year old married man devoted himself completely to the success of his business. His wife felt that her husband was losing track of her and their children. He kept rationalizing his need to have the business for the sake of his family. Once his wife had been diagnosed to have cancer of the breast, he was stunned. The thought of losing her was painful. He made an immediate turnaround and devoted more of his time to his wife and children.*

His wife's cancer was like a traumatic command to take another *real* look at his life. Not guilt, but the threat of loss compelled him to reacquaint himself with what was valuable to him. He reevaluated his priorities. As a result, a renewal took place. Once the cancer had been discovered, he took more and more time to be with his wife. Their dates were over long cups of coffee at which time they re-experienced their past together. With renewal, the successful dating of yesteryear become guides to discover new opportunities for change. In true unions, the trust and affection make "the going back" easier and more fruitful, for the essence of union is unabashed openness. "Going back" must be an orientation to a significant figure or an important idea, and making the orientation of life more meaningful must be the purpose. Scrooge did not conquer time by going back to his former fiancé Belle. The love for his dead sister Fan brought about his miracle of renewal. Reacquaintance is really a simple matter of getting in touch once more with old meaningful feelings and experiences. Reacquaintence is getting in touch with old feelings that once bonded relationships. Reacquaintance is an opportunity for rediscovery and renewal. In loose terms, renewal is making something better. In union, the man and woman have learned how to use dating as a means for reacquaintance and renewal.

Relaxed openness and the felt awareness of past experiences, now happy memories, are the crucial keys to fruitful dating. The specifics are not as important as keeping alive the hopeful, exciting expectations of the first date - that first, fresh beginning, when each tried to please and impress the other. Dating is a setting for a cozy climate of special intimacy. The whole idea is to transform the cross of burdensome marriage to a joyful journey. The transformation can only take place in selfless love. Reacquaintance carries the hope of the upward spiral toward union. Intimacy once gained and cherished can only grow into a larger dimension of accessibility and caring for. The important small talk of the renewals and the rediscoveries depend upon the realness of the intimacy.

Reacquaintance does serve the purpose of discovery, a glimpse of old patterns with the hope to change and to grow into the larger space of union. Life can become a humdrum ritual, and the discovery of old deadening patterns of relatedness must be dealt with in order to insure the opening of the circles of novelty.

A wife had made the observation that each year en route to family gatherings her husband would become testy and "picky." He would become irascible, and he would deny his behavior. At some point, en route to a family gathering, his wife chanced the observation that he did not like these gatherings. With much difficulty he admitted that these gatherings were boring and without meaning. He had projected his distaste on to his wife, and accused her of not wanting to be with his family. Once he made the connection, he changed the whole pattern. His life with his wife improved.

Discovery with a *meaningful* person is the key opening for "dating."

The point has been made that dating lends opportunities for giving from within the self and for making amends to the other. Dating is important because the deep down need to give transforms sex from the gonads to the core of the person, the heart. Libidinal transformation moves erotic, sexual relatedness into spiritual/transcendental experience. The energy of transformation is libido, or life force.

The sex of common parlance is fragmented, self-serving, and isolated. Standing by itself, sex collapses. Thoroughly consummated in transformation, sex becomes part of a much larger experience. Sex is then transformed into a human, spiritual force, and ceases to be a sexual act. The drive quality of sex becomes, or is transformed into a force referred to as libido. Libido is that force manifested in meaningful connections. Libido is neither desire nor pleasure. Libido is an energy that seeks and sustains life. In human consciousness, this life force can suffuse body senses, feeling-thoughts, and also objects of the outside world. This attachment or connecting up is libidinization. Libidinization makes the world breathe and grow. Libidinization swells the inner life and harmonizes thoughts and feelings into appropriate action. Libidinization brings color and depth to relationships, and consequently meaning. Libidinization brings things and people outside the self inside the self, and governs the unfolding of the whole self. Libidinization is crucial for the experience of intimacy. Libidinization rests upon innate temperamental factors as well as socio-psychological ones, such as the triangular exchanges with mother and father. The ability to love is part learned, and possibly part genetic. Indeed pleasure is the original moving force, but with differentiation of the self from the rest of the world, especially parents, the individual becomes much more aware of one's own need without loss of love of the other.

The need to love and be loved, often associated with the need for connectedness and beauty, sets the basis for future relationships. For marriage to become a union, sex must be transformed. Dating affords that opportunity for libidinal transformation.

CHAPTER VIII

The Transformation Of Marriage To Union

Libidinal transformation brings about a change in the nature of a relationship. The emotional fulfillment of a person is no longer directed to exclusive self-satisfaction, but to the needs and wants of another. Fulfillment is not found with oneself alone, but rather in closure with another. This connection is not random, but is an outgrowth of development and the experience of giving. In this way, a relationship gains history and meaning. The raw feelings of blind instinctual drives are changed into finely tuned feelings for another. Indeed raw feelings become the chord and the color of emotional relatedness, and touch all of emerging consciousness. The movement is from the self-indulgent "I" to the psychological emoting to another. Emotions are finely tuned feelings directed to another. This tuning involves thoughts, feelings, and dreams. Once emotions are shared a relationship has been created. And then the hard work begins.

The phases of transformation that I shall now discuss concern the man and woman. How these transformations may occur in homosexuals and the celibate, at this time I am not now equipped to discuss. I suspect that the love of another to the point of sacrifice is the key for all. The heterosexual transformation, has five phases:

PHASE I – DATING: EXPLORATION

As pointed out, the dating phase is made up of renewal, reacquaintance, and discovery. Dating sets the basis for mature sexual and sensual experience. This phase is not only social, but also harbors the "possibilities." Beginning in a visual way, there then arises the *desire* to touch, smell, and to be with. Attraction leads to a desire to incorporate – "I love you so much I could eat you." This attraction-incorporation must remain a basic aspect of marriage: to be close to; to take care of; to speak to; to have and to hold as precious as oneself. In marital dating, the tone of the first date must be kept alive and constantly renewed. The physical attraction of the first date which I call the ZING, must always be ingrained in the relationship, and must be accompanied by an openness and responsiveness. To achieve this state of being, affectionate regard is necessary, and this feeling takes one beyond the perceptual limits of the eye, especially as a husband and wife grow old. This relatedness comes about only to those who are able to give of themselves. Transformation requires a level of development that goes beyond the self, filled with as much affection as desire. Ideal? Possibly, but only such an exchange of affection brings relationships to the meaningful connections which are so crucial to marriage. Unions do not just happen. They are built. As pointed out, dating drops the draw-bridge. The other person must cease to be an object for dating to grow into union.

Phase II – First Contact: The Awakening

At some point, contact between two bodies takes place. If the relationship remains physical, the relationship will have a short life. Real love must flow from the deep center of oneself. The physical contact becomes the core of an emerging intimacy. Unfortunately this has been called *foreplay*. It is not *play*, nor is it *before* – it is the outgrowth of Phase I. In Phase II, the gates to one's deeper self are called upon to open and to share with the other. This phase is not a surrender, but much more an expression of faith, of desire to want to give, of a need to be in close physical contact with the other. Of course, this closeness sets off emotional reactions that in turn activate more physical reactions. If Phase I is the dropping of the drawbridge, then in Phase II, the husband and wife must encourage each other to cross that passageway to risk what rests on the other side. This phase requires much tenderness and caring. Two people must engage in the emotional crossing. Real love never develops on a one-way street. This risk is a two way one. This is a phase which requires good taste and patience, for each must drop shields and unmask masks. The private world of one becomes public to another.

Erogenous zones are important in the initial sexual encounters. To attain the joy of relatedness, one must gain access to that part of the other self that encourages trust, responsiveness, receptivity, and novelty. Repetition then is not necessarily compulsive routine, but can be a re-experiencing of pleasure and joyfulness. This phase subtly requires tenderness, great control, and constant awareness of the other. In this phase, couples can fool themselves and can confuse the sexual with the erotic and the sensual. For this reason many smutty jokes are directed at this phase, such as "an upper persuasion for a lower invasion!" The trust of Phase I can suffice to reinforce the psychological forces released in Phase II. Once this is achieved, Phase II never ends. Intimacy has begun.

PHASE III – THE ACT PROPER: "SEX"

If ever human encounter exposes people to intense vulnerability, this phase does. This phase is indeed much more than the discharge of sexual organs, although its appearance indicates that this is simply an act of pleasure. Above all, the act itself cannot be faked with impunity. Many think that they can fake it, and many do so unknowingly, only to pay the price of emptiness. Deprived of connectedness, the soul of meaningfulness is lost and the act shrivels. The act is a motoric act, an act requiring muscles, but needs an inner feeling spirit that brings it beyond the detumescence of organs. Suffused with pleasure to insure human continuity of the species, this sexual phenomenon can only be sustained by affection and caring. Attraction draws the couple together, but two souls must meld in a tender, non-verbal manner. In Tantra, this attraction is depicted as the "meeting of the eyes."

As much as human beings depend on pleasure for survival, in the same way they must develop and live a sense of a larger destiny, a destiny beyond the physical needs of the self. When meaning gains direction, human action takes on the quality of continuity. The sexual act becomes a creative act only when two people take on the full responsibility for the act. The sexual experience is not only creative in its continuation of a species, but also harbors a give-ness potential. The act can transform a couple into one, and a marriage into a union. Since the act is so phenomenally physical, the deeper psychological and spiritual roots are not readily discernable, nor easily appreciated. All attempts to exaggerate the fervor of the experience are doomed to distortion and perversion of the act. Sexual fulfillment is intimate, the sharing of deep feelings and concern for another. The sense of one's own worth however is a crucial pre-requisite before any sharing can take place. The sexual act proper is not about a series of different erotic adventures. The sexual act should be about deepening affection, and ironically, in such cases, the experience does become erotic. At such a time, the state of union has been touched.

93

Phase IV – Post-Coital: Reconstitution

This phase is the moment when the self returns to itself, a moment clearer and sharper in focus. A time when the mind becomes limpid. All the feelings, actions, hopes, and dreams of a person then return to the reality of the world. The bright light of fulfillment dispels the darkness of just physical sex. The world of the self, of the *now*, seeks the vertical spiral of the transcendental self. The tenderness and quiet good will of dating become the transforming factors. The post-coital phase must not be jarred by smoking a cigarette or eating a sandwich. The other person must not be extruded. The pearls of the experience must be threaded into a whole. The self must return slowly and silently to itself.

Neither husband nor wife should leave the other out. The caring attentiveness must be carried over to the next moment. In this way, a sense of worth and value reinforces the relationship. These four phases are much like light that holds all the colors of the rainbow. In true love, there are all the people that one has ever loved, and the act of caring is the vessel from which all love is poured.

Phase V – The Next Day: Fulfillment

The "next day" is not to be taken in a literal way. The "next day" is a metaphor for the future of the relationship. The "next day" holds the hope which caresses the couple in a harsh world. The "next day" holds the potential for a springboard burst of growth and renewed energy. For a marriage to become a union, an enlightened spirit is necessary, enlightened, in that it sees the old experiences with new possibilities and a renewed spirit, which goes beyond the physical. In music, a musician cannot just play the notes; he must play the notes in the context of his esthetic interpretation of the entire work. This "next day" experience is not only attained through the "sexual" aspect of marriage, but can also be attained whenever people arrive at the true sharing of oneself with another.

In preparation for mystical experiences, meditation is necessary. Meditation frees one of all distraction in order to empty the person's mind of those inconsequential things that can interfere with the necessary inward focus. This emptying, kenosis, brings the person out of the world of the senses to one beyond the senses, the transcendental world. In marriage, true "sex" is the emptying experience that transports the marriage to the potential of the transcendental "next day" to become union.

The sexual act can be used, and is very often used, for exclusive pleasure. This is indeed part of the real world. To ignore its deeper meaning, as is so easily done, one can readily miss the potential destruction its aimless pursuit can bring about. Boredom and anger feed "pure" sex. Everything in this world and in this universe stands in relationship to another thing. As with anything else which stands alone, sex for its own sake is a dead end and leads to listless ennui. Emotional fulfillment so necessary to human beings can only be found in the sacrificing exchange between two people. Since the sexual act contains the potential power of creation, respect for this given power cannot be distorted merely to a self-end.

Prostitution represents the pure act of "what for what," and indicates how "sex" can be twisted in any utilitarian direction. Human beings can be moved in any direction of their want. For this reason, vigilance is necessary to avoid the corruption of the beauty of what "sex" could become. No doubt the sexual act "proper" is suffused with exquisite pleasure, and it is this pleasure that overcomes human sloth to insure the survival of the species. The prodding rod that is pleasure must be turned into a transforming spirit by directing concupiscent desire into caring for another. The act then is no longer *just* physical. Love is true caring that bridges the human gaps, and sacrifice so necessary in love transforms a physical act into one beyond the senses. Without affection and caring, the sexual act becomes mired in cement. Biology is only one aspect of the human experience. For the "next day" to be grounded in joy and meaning, the biological imperative must be transformed into the spirit of union. Exclusive biology in the human experience leads to perversity.

> *A married man had a library of pornographic films. His wife's complaint was that he neglected her and was caught up in his own satisfaction. He spent his time watching these films, but never "tried any of that stuff with me."*

In the transcendental realm, the "next day" becomes part of an ever-renewing cycle of energy, not only as a personal experience, but as much for the other. Relatedness must be nurtured, especially by tenderness and trust. For marriage to become a union there must be a constant reforming of the relationship. In this way, the best of a marital relationship is prepared to greet those "next days."

CHAPTER IX

The "Next Day"

For a relationship to become whole or complete, to permit the other to enter one's inner world, one's mind and soul, is a daunting task. This is a human undertaking fraught with much risk. Almost all of what makes up life seems to conspire against the melding of the core of one with that of another. The "next day" is taken to be the moment to integrate the frayed aspects of marriage into a union. Boredom and apathy create a tolerant familiarity, a warm frozenness wherein each takes the other for granted.

In a routinized relationship, life becomes hardened into meaningless ritual, and life is lived for that day which never could come. Santa Claus and wishing upon stars do not bring passion into relationships. The hope of tomorrows rests within the self. Dating rests on those "next days." Temperament serves the shaping of individual psychology, and as pointed out, temperamental differences between two can be bridged by the affectionate regard of one for the other. In this way, understanding and sharing interests of the other molds a meaningful union. This kind of attentiveness should never be used as a bargaining chip to get what one wants. Bartered love is prostitution. Real caring bridges the temperamental gulfs, and without knowing, individual horizons are raised.

Differences unite when there is trust, affection, spontaneity, and an openness in exchange. The desire to know what differences must be brought into harmony is crucial. Such a working through requires a leap and is not one for the moment. Hopeful marriage is never sensational, never aroused simply by the senses, the superficial emotion or moment. Hopeful marriage is transcendental, beyond the senses and does not belong to the world of things. Real death takes place in the heart. Real caring shares timelessness with the Universe. Life can only be sustained by honest connections, and such connections once strung together, not only give meaning to a relationship, but lend direction to life and its appreciation. Unions take place. In such a state of being, the space of the Universe is no longer a daunting vision for the human being, for the love that characterizes union *is* of the very silent substance of the Universe. Already, space walks are full of wonder and *caritas* for our earth. The grand splendor of the human being is attained in true giving, and this splendor is manifested in the courage of loving, like Spring always returning in its silent way with its fragile beauty. Spring endures with a freshness. Dating encourages those "next days" that are crucial for human beings to find each other, and in this way they sight what hope is made of.

Recently, scientists have described another form of matter to join the solid and gas. In this new form, the Boise-Einstein condensate, individual atoms collect the wave-lengths of other atoms and form an overlap. They create a kind of "super" atom that then forms a cloud! In the same sense, dating is a collecting of all the "next days," to form that center that holds the whole to be greater than the sum of its parts. That is what love is. No central core is lost, but rather the basis is set for a three-fold cord to be born of two.

The demands of human relatedness are so outrageous that for a marriage to emerge into something much more than a St. Valentine's Card demands a constant groping and exchanging of good will. The feeling of caring for the other and knowing the other must be constantly rekindled. The visions of individual horizons become much more intimately overlapped into one, without loss of the self. "Super" atom! "Super" person! Such people are those of character, those of integrity and moral responsibility. They are not people of the shiny moment.

True dating is then a special time between two friends. True dating is about a couple who *need* to share a special feeling. The fulfillment of that need creates kindred spirits. In my private practice when I would engage husbands in a half joking manner to "date your wife," they would look at me in shocked bewilderment. Most people forget, or have never learned the importance of enjoying small, familiar moments, never to be taken for granted. Marriage en route to union does not need rising mists, acrobatic sex, or ringing bells. Real marriage requires tenderness and openness, and takes place in the quiet hope of the small things. As Madame Butterfly says, "Noi siamo i genti delle piccole cose" (we are people of the small things). The "right" car, the "right" home, the "right" vacation, the "right" setting – there is no "right" anything! One must listen to the other from within the self. Marriage requires friendship, and the sharing of the small things.

The "next day" sets the stage for the dating to be joyous. The flatness of a date in marriage is related to its dying roots, the *sharing* of the small things. Dating is a sensitive indicator about the state of marriage. The "next day" becomes a link to all the days of the marriage and to one's ancient past that makes the present day a part of the past. Love is not divisible. When one loves one, one loves all those whom one has ever loved.

The "next day" requires the woman to be as receptive and responsive as she was during the Phase III of "Sex." To be receptive means to be open to the good intentions of the other with no preconceived idea of what is expected. In being responsive, women must bring their feelings to the moment. A passive woman is not active in a relationship, and should not be confused with a woman of passivity. A woman of passivity is active in her own right, as she is when she chooses to become pregnant. She makes an *active* choice to put her body and mind in harm's way. In such a case, this is not a passive experience in which she does nothing. Her choice is an active one. She is actively involved in her choices to have a child and to care for one. In the same way during the sexual act, she must bring herself actively to her husband. The woman of passivity is assertive in a feminine way: not for her ego, but rather for the fulfillment of her inner human need. The passive woman surrenders to adaptation; the woman of passivity does not try to win, but acts to complete her nature by bringing closure to her nature by remaining in tune with Nature.

In essence, men must do the same, and must bring an energy, a tenderness, and a courage to their desire. Openness and responsiveness must fashion their willingness to bring devotion and affection to know women beyond their ego satisfaction. Men must convince women that they mean "I'm yours - you're mine! Forevermore!" Ideal? Perhaps, but worthwhile to labor for. The climate that men create must be one of active involvement and courage, never one of self-pity. They must become active listeners to their wives about those things important *to her.* As much as a woman enters the experience of passivity, so too at times must he. The masculine friendship of the men's club, or of the sports bar can be important for men, but friendship for a wife is much dearer, for it is forged in patient open listening and giving. This kind of friendship can take place at the Super Bowl, at the opera, in the kitchen.

The "next day" experience must be lived by both husband and wife, the husband initiating and the wife actively responding. At times, the other way around. The husband and wife must bear the same intentionality toward each other and life. They must never fence over issues, and there can be no moments of dour disenchantments of "is this all there is?" To become honest in marriage requires working at every moment of the marriage. Corrections are constantly being made, and when they are meaningful, the relationship becomes a rising spiral of circles, always popping open to what is new and fresh. Never closed, always open. Never the hint of boredom.

Dating offers the opportunity for that imaginative consciousness wherein differences become catalysts to distill the relationship to become one of esteemed affection. Only in this way can marriage become a union, and the "next days" become the substance to be transformed.

> *A professional woman was in emotional doldrums concerning her practice. She did not say a word. Her husband sensed her state of mind. He told her to spiffy up and took her for a walk in Soho. Her spirits were lifted, and she was refreshed.*

That is imaginative consciousness at its best. That is a great *date.*

EPILOGUE

In conclusion, my contention is that marriage is a developmental phase of life to rest ultimately in union. Two become one flesh. The unfolding of a good relationship becomes a union. For this emergence, there must be the endless work of selfless giving. This giving is not conditional – it is not *quid pro quo*: "You give me and I shall give you." The giving is reciprocal, one hundred percent both ways. I have called this phenomenon, a resonant narcissism, or loving the other as much as one loves oneself. The energy indeed stems from self-love and is transmitted to the other through the experience of what has been called *dating*. These dates are then strung together by the energy of "the next day."

In marriage, there must emerge a harmony of differences. The temperamental differences and the incompatibilities can be brought into a harmony when there is a mutual deep caring and respect. In an open-minded relationship, a seemingly chaotic situation can be turned into the paradox of growth: without death there can be no life; without loss, there can be no love. Faith carries the hope of the fulfillment of things unseen.

Rapprochement of differences with all their paradoxical possibilities are embedded in language. The word *precarious,* for example, means dependent on chance circumstances, and the word *prayer* means a petition to a Divinity. Yet both words have the same Latin root *precarius* that means obtained by entreaty or prayer. In the same strange way, as pointed out before, the group of slaves in the Roman household, the *familia*, became the *famiglia,* the stronghold of later Italian culture. Irony is a strange part of hope.

The catalyst for union is the intimacy of knowing and appropriate responding. I once saw a program about grizzlies and two naturalists, a man and a woman. Unafraid, they stood before these huge creatures. The naturalists had learned how bears functioned, and were able to be in their presence face-to-face, without weapons and without fear. No violence occurred. Trust developed. Fear would have been interpreted as an attack. This is the kind of trust, knowing, and intuition that are crucial in marital transformation.

The key to this transformation of love from marriage to union is the imperative to deal with the dread of loss of a loved one, with no fear of "loss" of the self in caring for another. For love to grow, for energy to expand, there must be an exchange between and among people. In this case of marriage – union, there are two people. The "sex" of marriage must be libidinized into the giving of the self in "the next day." One form of energy is turned upward to a higher form: more complex, more organized, more unseen. Perhaps this is what was expressed in Ecclesiastes: that the two-fold cord of marriage would become a three-fold cord. Who is the other in this strange equation of $1 + 1 = 3$? Libidinization is a state of being in which a person transcends the needs and wants of the biological self. A person tries to perfect the self by going beyond biological roots to those of the spirit – from a solipsistic narcissism ("I love me") to a resonant narcissism ("I love you as I love myself"). This state of being may be reached through the fulfillment of carnal (sexual) appetites, social-religious sacrifices, or both. Indeed a union grows out of the libidinization of love.

> *But since human life is a fragile and unstable thing we have no choice but to be ever on the search for people whom we may love, and by whom we may be loved in turn, for if charity and good will are removed from life, all the joy is gone out of it. (Cicero, On Friendship)*

Marriage – union is the closest thing to heaven on this earth. So "date your wife" and enjoy your "next days!"

Bibliography

Cicero, *On Friendship*. ed. H. E. Gould and J.L. Whiteley. Illinois: Bolchazy-Carducci Publishers, Inc., 1999.

Whitman, Walt. *Leaves of Grass*. ed. Sculley Bradley and Harold Blodgett. New York: W. W. Norton, 1973.

NOTES

Salvatore V. Ambrosino, M.D.

SALVATORE V. AMBROSINO, M.D.

This edition of *Date Your Wife* is the first text by CAMB Publishing to be published in a Print on Demand forum through Xlibris Press.
The text was designed by Patty Wolff,
Jacqueline Leone, and the staff at Xlibris Press.
It was set in AGaramond typeface.

Printed in the United States
2014